Agile Scrum Handbook – 3rd edition

Other publications by Van Haren Publishing

Van Haren Publishing (VHP) specializes in titles on Best Practices, methods and standards within four domains:
- IT and IT Management
- Architecture (Enterprise and IT)
- Business Management and
- Project Management

Van Haren Publishing is also publishing on behalf of leading organizations and companies: ASLBiSL Foundation, BRMI, CA, Centre Henri Tudor, CATS CM, Gaming Works, IACCM, IAOP, IFDC, Innovation Value Institute, IPMA-NL, ITSqc, NAF, KNVI, PMI-NL, PON, The Open Group, The SOX Institute.

Topics are (per domain):

IT and IT Management	Enterprise Architecture	Business Management
ABC of ICT	ArchiMate®	*BABOK® Guide*
ASL®	GEA®	BiSL® and BiSL® Next
CMMI®	Novius Architectuur	BRMBOK™
COBIT®	Methode	BTF
e-CF	TOGAF®	CATS CM®
ISO/IEC 20000		DID®
ISO/IEC 27001/27002	**Project Management**	EFQM
ISPL	A4-Projectmanagement	eSCM
IT4IT®	DSDM/Atern	IACCM
IT-CMF™	ICB / NCB	ISA-95
IT Service CMM	ISO 21500	ISO 9000/9001
ITIL®	MINCE®	OPBOK
MOF	M_o_R®	SixSigma
MSF	MSP®	SOX
SABSA	P3O®	SqEME®
SAF	*PMBOK® Guide*	
SIAM™	Praxis®	
TRIM	PRINCE2®	
VeriSM™		

For the latest information on VHP publications, visit our website: www.vanharen.net.

Agile Scrum Handbook

3rd edition

Nader K. Rad

Colophon

Title:	Agile Scrum Handbook – 3rd edition
Author:	Nader K. Rad
Text editor:	Stephen Brightman
Publisher:	Van Haren Publishing, 's-Hertogenbosch-NL, www.vanharen.net
DTP:	Coco Bookmedia, Amersfoort
ISBN Hard copy:	978 94 018 0759 3
ISBN eBook (pdf):	978 94 018 0760 9
ISBN ePUB:	978 94 018 0761 6
Edition:	Third edition, first impression, April 2021
Copyright:	Nader K. Rad & Van Haren Publishing

For further information on Van Haren Publishing, e-mail to: info@vanharen.net.

Copyright:
All rights reserved. No part of this publication may be reproduced in any form by print, photo print, microfilm or any other means without written permission by the publisher.

Trademark notices
DSDM® is a registered trademark of Agile Business Consortium Limited.
ITIL®, MOV®, MSP®, PRINCE2® and PRINCE2 Agile® are registered trademarks of AXELOS Limited.
PMBOK® Guide is a registered trademark of The Project Management Institute, Inc.
Nexus™ is a trademark of Scrum.org.
Scrum@Scale™ is a trademark of Scrum Inc.
LeSS™ is a trademark of The LeSS Company B.V.
SAFe™ is a trademark of Scaled Agile Inc.

Contents

1. THE AGILITY CONCEPT 1

   1.1   The Development Approaches 2
          1.1.1   The predictive approach 2
          1.1.2   The adaptive approach 4
   1.2   Selecting a Development Approach 8
   1.3   Is Agile Only Suitable for IT Development? 9
          1.3.1   Projects 9
          1.3.2   Programs 10
          1.3.3   Operations 10
   1.4   Is Agile Faster? 10
   1.5   Is Agile New? 11

2. SCRUM 13

   2.1   Scrum as a Framework 13
   2.2   Scrum as a Wrapper 14
   2.3   The Scrum Structure 14
          2.3.1   People 15
          2.3.2   Events 24
          2.3.3   Artifacts 36
   2.4   Scaled Scrum 46
          2.4.1   Roles 47
          2.4.2   Events 49
          2.4.3   Artifacts 51

3. CRYSTAL 53

- 3.1 The Cockburn Scale 53
- 3.2 Frequent Release 54
- 3.3 Osmotic Communication 54
- 3.4 Walking Skeleton 55
- 3.5 Information Radiators 55
  - 3.5.1 Escaped defects 57
  - 3.5.2 Progress information 58
  - 3.5.3 Niko-Niko calendar 63

4. EXTREME PROGRAMMING 65

- 4.1 Daily Routine 65
  - 4.1.1 Pairing 65
  - 4.1.2 Assignment 66
  - 4.1.3 Design 66
  - 4.1.4 Write test 67
  - 4.1.5 Code 67
  - 4.1.6 Refactor 68
  - 4.1.7 Integrate 68
  - 4.1.8 Go home! 69
  - 4.1.9 Stand-up meetings 69
  - 4.1.10 Tracking 69
  - 4.1.11 Risk management 69
- 4.2 Spiking 70
- 4.3 The Nature of Items 70
  - 4.3.1 The two rules 71
  - 4.3.2 INVEST 72
  - 4.3.3 User stories 72
- 4.4 Estimating 74
  - 4.4.1 Ideal-time 74
  - 4.4.2 Story points 76
  - 4.4.3 T-shirt sizes 77
  - 4.4.4 Velocity 78
  - 4.4.5 Planning poker 82
  - 4.4.6 Triangulation 85
  - 4.4.7 Affinity estimation 86
  - 4.4.8 Re-estimating 87
- 4.5 Feedback loops 87
- 4.6 The Planning Onion 89

5. DSDM® 91
- 5.1 Project Constraints 92
- 5.2 Upfront Planning 93
- 5.3 MoSCoW Prioritization 94
- 5.4 Exceptions 95
- 5.5 Self-Organization 95
- 5.6 Contract Types 96

6. KANBAN 97
- 6.1 Visualizing 97
- 6.2 Limiting WIP 98
- 6.3 Pull vs. Push 99

7. PHILOSOPHIZING! 105
- 7.1 eXtreme Programming Ideas 105
  - 7.1.1 Customer bill of rights 105
  - 7.1.2 Programmer bill of rights 107
  - 7.1.3 Values 109
- 7.2 DSDM® Ideas 110
  - 7.2.1 Philosophy 110
  - 7.2.2 Principles 111
- 7.3 Scrum Ideas 113
  - 7.3.1 Pillars 113
  - 7.3.2 Values 114
- 7.4 The Agile Manifesto 115
  - 7.4.1 Statement #1 115
  - 7.4.2 Statement #2 116
  - 7.4.3 Statement #3 116
  - 7.4.4 Statement #4 117
  - 7.4.5 The Principles 117

ABOUT THE AUTHOR 121

INDEX 123

1. The Agility Concept

There are many myths and misleading concepts about Agile, starting with the answer to the most basic question in this context: **What is Agile?**

What you may often hear is ambiguous statements such as "Agile is a mindset". Agile, like almost everything else, **needs** a particular mindset, but it's not correct to say that Agile **is** a mindset. Saying that "Agile is a mindset" has only one practical consequence: It lets certain people do whatever they want and just call it Agile because it's fashionable these days.

Another common problem in our community is the illusion of the external enemy. Those of you familiar with the way authoritarian systems work know that they always need to have an enemy. It helps cover the gaps they have in their system by creating distractions, and creates a common goal to cover the lack of real, achievable internal goals. It's sad to see that many Agile practitioners have the same approach, usually for the personal gain of a few *leaders*.

It's best for your professional life to be open to different ideas and learn from all of them without you becoming a cult member. This approach is the first principle in the Nearly Universal Principles of Projects: https://nupp.guide

So, let's start by talking about the real nature of Agile.

1.1 The Development Approaches

When you're developing a piece of software, the following steps are done in one way or another, either for separate features or for the solution as a whole:
- Analyze
- Design
- Construct
- Integrate
- Test

You can, of course, use other names for these steps, merge them into fewer steps, or split them into more – that's all fine. These steps can be called **delivery processes**, which are different from management processes such as planning and monitoring.

So how are you going to arrange and run these processes? Think about a few options before reading the rest of this chapter.

1.1.1 The predictive approach
You probably have a few options in mind, and they all belong to one of the two generic forms, which we will discuss next. Each of these options can be called a **development lifecycle** or a **development approach**.

The next figure shows one generic development lifecycle.

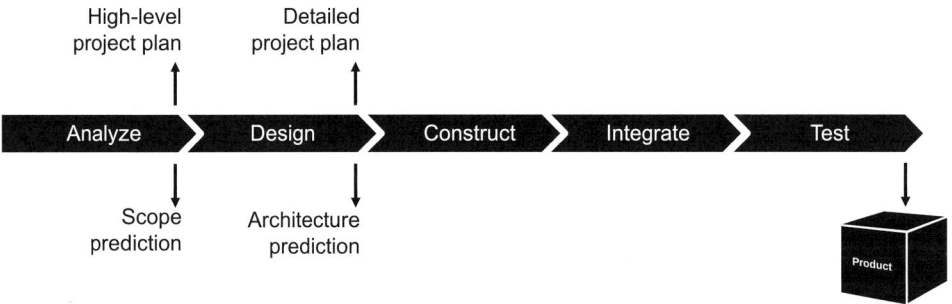

In this lifecycle, each process is completed before we proceed to the next one:
1. First, we completely analyze the requirements and decide what we want to have in the solution.
2. We then design the architecture of the whole solution and find out the best way to form the features.
3. Programmers then start building the units.
4. The units are then integrated into one solution.
5. Finally, the solution is fully tested and errors are fixed.

Obviously, the steps can overlap; e.g., you don't need to wait until all units are complete before integrating and testing them. As a result, the same lifecycle would look like the following figure with overlaps:

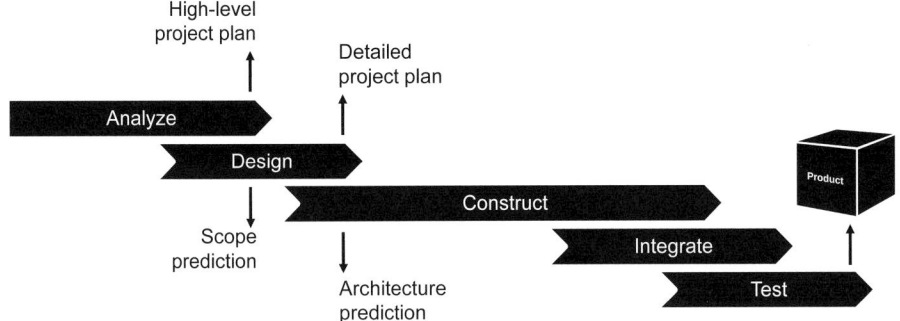

This is not fundamentally different from the previous lifecycle, as we still have a sequence of development processes as the main driver.

This type of lifecycle is based on an initial investigation to understand what we need to produce. We have an upfront specification, an upfront design, and consequently, an upfront plan. That's why some people call it **plan-driven development**. Furthermore, we try to predict what we need and how it can be produced, and that's why a common name for it is **predictive development**.

Predictive lifecycles are the normal and appropriate way to develop many types of projects, such as construction. You plan and design first, and then follow those optimized, well-formed plans and designs. However, this is not a comfortable way of working in some projects, such as typical IT development projects. You can spend a lot of time specifying and analyzing the requirements, and then base everything else on that. What happens next, though? The customer won't be happy when they see the result! They will ask for changes, and changes are expensive in this lifecycle because you may have to revise all the previous work.

As it's commonly remarked in the IT industry, the customer doesn't know what they want until they see the product. But when do they see the product in a predictive lifecycle? Towards the end of the project – at which point, the cost of change is at its maximum.

The Agile community usually refers to predictive systems as **waterfall** systems. However, it's not a good idea to use this term because it has developed a negative connotation, and its use would bias an otherwise rational conversation about the development approaches.

1.1.2 The adaptive approach

To overcome the problems that IT development projects have with predictive lifecycles, we can sacrifice the comfort and structure of a predictive system and use a different lifecycle that creates the product incrementally, to check it with the customers and end-users along the way. This is a luxury we have in IT development projects that not everyone else has. Think about a construction project: There are no meaningful increments for it, and the product is not usable until the end.

To be fair, this disadvantage of construction projects (where we can't build them incrementally) is balanced with the fact that if you start a project to build a hospital, it doesn't matter how many changes you make, the final result will be a hospital, and not, for example, a theme park! However, in IT development, you may indeed start a project to create something like a hospital and end up with something like a theme park.

So, based on the fact that we can have incremental delivery in IT development projects, let's exploit this opportunity with a lifecycle like the on in the next figure.

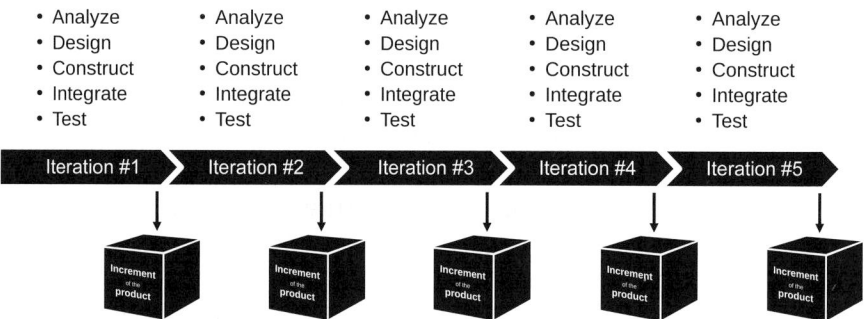

There's no real prediction in this lifecycle, as instead of predicting the product and relying on that prediction, we have short iterations in which we create increments of the product. Each iteration is focused on a few features that seem promising. We build each one, show the increment to the customer and end-users, receive their feedback, and decide what to do in the next iteration. So, instead of predicting, we carry on with the project and **adapt** to the feedback. This approach uses an **adaptive lifecycle**. "Agile" is the popular name for adaptive systems.

To create each increment, we need to iterate through all the development processes during each time window, and that's why we call those windows **iterations**, and this way of development **iterative development**. In iterative development, each process (such as design) is repeated multiple times for different elements in the product, instead of being run once for the whole product.

Normally, iterative development and incremental delivery occur together.

1.1.2.1 Fixed-scope vs. fixed-duration iterations
In your opinion, is it better to have fixed-scope iterations or fixed-duration ones?

Theoretically, both of them can work, but in practice, fixed-duration iterations are superior, because keeping the scope of the iteration fixed, can have the following results:
- You may spend too much time on each feature and add too many bells and whistles. Having a fixed duration continuously pushes you to focus on the most valuable things first.
- The time you need to complete the scope is usually longer than you expect, which makes the iterations longer and reduces the number of feedback loops. When there's less feedback, there will be less adaptation.

So, that's why almost all Agile methods have fixed-duration iterations, and they usually insist on respecting these **timeboxes**. A timebox is a window with a maximum (or fixed) amount of time, which isn't extended under any circumstances (because if you extend it once, you will do it all the time).

1.1.2.2 Duration of iterations
Now that the iterations are supposed to be timeboxed, how long should that be for?

We can receive feedback at any time, but the structured feedback we receive at the end of each iteration is key. Therefore, shorter iterations give us more structured feedback, and therefore, more opportunities for adaptation. On the other hand, each iteration needs to have enough time to produce a number of features worthy of a serious review with the customer, which means that they can't be too short.

In the early days of the Agile systems, 4 to 8 weeks seems like a good idea. Nowadays, shorter durations are more acceptable. The maximum acceptable duration is 4 weeks in most systems, and durations as short as 1 week seem practical for the current technologies.

1.1.2.3 Same duration or different durations
In your opinion, is it better to have the same duration for all iterations, or to keep them flexible?

Having the same duration is more disciplined and instills regularity. In most cases, there's no real need to decide about the duration of each timebox separately, which is why most systems set the same duration for all iterations. You can revise this timeboxed duration, but you won't decide about the duration of each iteration separately.

1.1.2.4 What happens inside iterations?
An iteration is a period of time in which we repeat the development processes. How do you do that, though?

Here are the two possibilities:

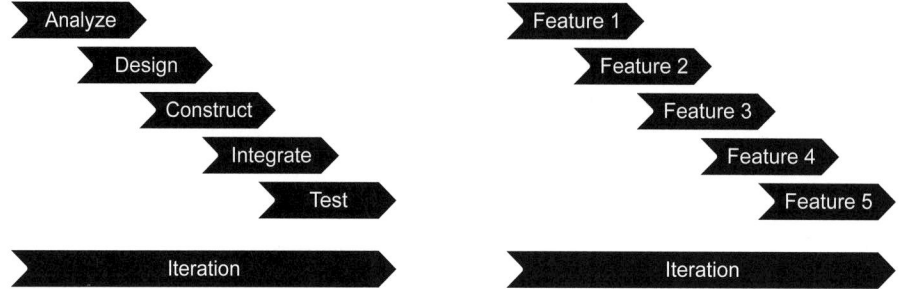

The one on the left goes through the development processes and runs each of them for all the features that belong to the iteration. Maybe we can call it mini-predictive.

The one on the right goes through the features, one or a few at a time, and runs all the development processes for each of them. We can consider it a mini-mini-predictive system (i.e., almost not predictive).

We prefer the second, feature-based option, mainly because it's the one that's compatible with timeboxed iterations.

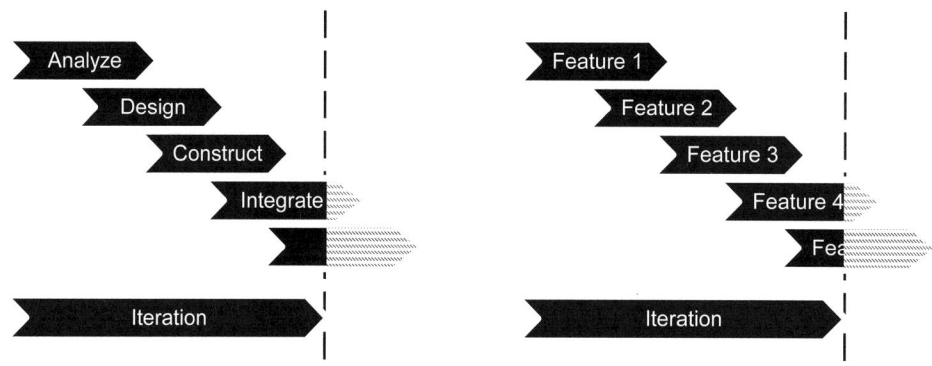

When there's a maximum duration, we may not be done with everything at the end of the iteration, which means that with the feature-based approach there are a few features we won't be done with, while with the other approach, we won't be done with one or more of the development processes of each of the features, which means that we won't have any usable output at the end of the iteration and we won't be able to demonstrate it and receive feedback.

1.1.2.5 Increment vs. deliverable

Each increment is a deliverable, but not every deliverable is an increment.

We use the term "increment" to refer to the increments of the product, which are, in the case of IT development, different versions of working software. Each new increment is a usable version of the same product but with more features, and it has to be usable to enable reliable feedback.

In contrast, a deliverable can be almost anything you produce in your project. For example, in a predictive project, the upfront design and upfront plan are deliverables that can't be considered increments of the product.

Since being Agile is fashionable, some people just call their deliverables increments and claim to be Agile based on that.

1.1.2.6 Iterations vs. cycles

Every iteration is a cycle, but not every cycle is an iteration.

An iteration is a special type of cycle wherein we repeat our **development processes** as well as our **management processes**. Many systems have cycles, but those cycles only repeat the management processes and not necessarily the development processes. The big, monthly cycle and the small, weekly cycle in P3.express, the stages in PRINCE2®, and the phases in the PMBOK® Guide are all examples of that.

To make this difference clearer, imagine a cycle that has its own planning, monitoring and controlling, and closing. The fact that these managerial processes are repeated is the reason their containers are called cycles. Now, imagine it's a predictive project, and one cycle is about specifying the requirements, the next cycle is about designing the product, and so on. This is a cyclic system without any iterations.

Unfortunately, some people think that as long as they can identify cycles in their projects, they can call them iterative and hence Agile, which is not correct. Even worse than mistaking managerial processes for development processes, some people just call arbitrary time periods in their projects iterations, and consider, for example, weekly "iterations" when there's no real iteration of any processes in them.

1.1.2.7 Testing and quality in agile

The following diagram shows an over-simplified schema of the way testing is done in each approach:

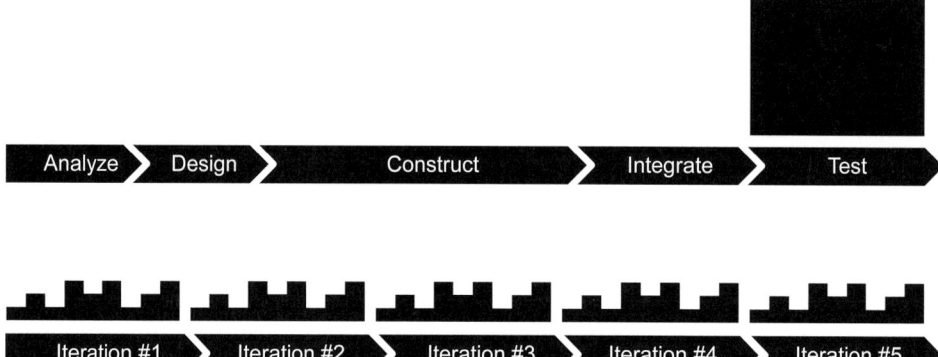

Most of the testing activities are at the end of a predictive project, which is when we're probably late and under a lot of pressure to finish the project as soon as possible. This pressure may result in dropping some of the tests and compromising on quality.

How about adaptive systems, then?

Well, this problem doesn't exist in adaptive lifecycles because testing is done continuously, and so it doesn't matter when we stop the project, as we will always have the right ratio of testing.

There are other differences also. For example, the nature of adaptive systems makes it almost essential to have automated tests. Automated tests may not cover every single line of code, and there's an optimum **test code coverage** that we need to have in our project. Test code coverage is the ratio of the lines of code tested by automated tests to the total number of lines.

1.2 Selecting a Development Approach

Each of the predictive and adaptive lifecycles has advantages and disadvantages. The right choice depends on many factors, but the most important one is the nature of the product.

You should ask two essential questions before deciding about the type of lifecycle you need for your project:
1. **Does it need to be adaptive?** If you don't need to be adaptive, a predictive lifecycle is more straightforward, more structured, and more *predictive*. An adaptive system

is needed when there is a risk of starting with the idea of creating something like a hospital and ending up with something like a theme park.
2. **Can it be adaptive?** This question is even more important than the previous one. To be adaptive, you must have the possibility of developing iteratively and delivering incrementally in order to receive feedback and adapt. Let's think of a construction project once again: Can you design the building iteratively? For example, can you design the foundation of the building without designing the rest of it, which is needed to determine the amount of load on the foundation? The answer is simply no. It's not possible to have iterative development (with the meaning we have for it in this context) for a construction project. Furthermore, incremental delivery is not possible in most situations because, on the one hand, the subsets of a building are not usable, and on the other hand, the feedback generated by one subset may not be applicable to the rest. So, we can't use an adaptive lifecycle to build a building (although, don't confuse this with interior design and decoration, or even renovation, for which we may be able to use an adaptive system).

The main message is that the decision between a predictive and an adaptive approach is not simply a matter of good and evil, but rather it depends on several factors. They are both valid approaches, and each of them is more suited to some types of product.

For practice, think about an IT project for upgrading the operating systems of 300 computers in an organization, or an IT project for creating a networking infrastructure for a very large organization with offices in six locations. In your opinion, which type of development lifecycle is more suitable for these two projects?

1.3 Is Agile Only Suitable for IT Development?

Most of the examples in this book, as well as other resources about Agile, are about IT development projects. Does that mean that Agile is limited to IT development projects?

1.3.1 Projects
There are some people who claim that Agile can be used for every type of project, and the same people usually claim that it's the only correct way of doing projects. They are usually people who have not experienced any serious project other than non-critical IT development ones. In reality, there are many types of project where an adaptive method is either not needed or not possible because we can't develop them iteratively and deliver them incrementally.

Aside from the simple fact that Agile is not the one absolute truth and cannot be used in every project, we can still consider the range of projects that can benefit from an adaptive system. Is it limited to IT development, or are there other suitable types?

It may be possible to use Agile in some other types of project, but it requires a professional, structured effort, which doesn't seem to have been done yet. There are some non-IT projects that claim to be Agile, but they usually mistake the meaning of Agility and are victims of the **Cargo Cult** effect. Notwithstanding this, IT development will probably remain the best type of project for adaptive methods.

1.3.2 Programs

Everything said so far has been about **projects**, but things are different when it comes to **programs**. According to MSP®, which is a program management method from the same family as PRINCE2® and ITIL®, projects may be either adaptive or predictive, but programs always have to be adaptive. This is so because projects are about products, while programs are about results. We can predict how to build products, but we can't predict how to achieve results.

1.3.3 Operations

Project management methods always start by defining what a project is, because they are only applicable to projects and not to programs, portfolios, or business as usual (operations). This has never become a tradition in Agile systems – they don't insist on being used in projects, and some people have been using them in operations. This has its roots in IT development, where there's no clear line between projects (major changes) and operations, where minor changes are applied to the product. The extreme version of this notion is visible in DevOps, where the project side (development) and business as usual side (operations) are merged into one.

1.4 Is Agile Faster?

The word "agile" implies that these methods are faster. While it is very difficult to confirm or reject this hypothesis, there's one concept that really helps in Agile projects, and it's not about the speed with which we develop, but about the set of features we need to develop (the scope).

Think of an IT project that is supposed to be developed using a predictive method. One or a few customer representatives would be responsible for identifying and communicating the requirements. They know that if they miss a requirement, it will be expensive and troubling to add them in the future, and therefore, they do their best to identify all requirements. As it turns out, they become too creative in this area and add requirements that add insufficient value. These extra features require more time and resources, and also make the product more complicated, which is a serious problem for future maintenance and expansions.

In an adaptive system, on the other hand, the customer representatives are not forced to come up with all the requirements upfront, and the chances are therefore lower that strange requirements will be added to the list. Even when there are such requirements, a proper adaptive development system at least helps the representatives understand their value so they can leave them for last, or even remove them.

In practice, an Agile project that is run properly has the chance of having a smaller scope, which makes the project faster and less complicated.

As an example, in 2002, Standish Group reported the following rate of use for the features of four of their internal applications:

```
Always used:      7%
Often used:      13%
Sometimes used:  16%
Rarely used:     19%
Never used:      45%
```

Imagine how much faster their projects could have been, and how much simpler their products could have been, if those never-used and rarely-used features had not been included. This is, of course, only one example of a few applications in one organization, but the overall trend may not be so different.

1.5 Is Agile New?

Agile is usually advertised as the new approach. The use of the term "Agile" to refer to adaptive lifecycles is certainly new, but what about the lifecycle itself?

It's difficult to imagine a long history of human beings with many projects and programs that have been done without any form of adaptive lifecycles. Think of a very popular type of initiative (project or program) in the olden days: going to war. Could you manage to wage a war using a predictive approach? Did they plan and design everything at the beginning? Certainly not. You may have a high-level plan (which is more like a strategy than a plan) and manage the war one battle (iteration) at a time, and based on the outcome of each battle, adapt for the rest of the initiative. It's not a pleasant example, but a clear one that shows that adaptive lifecycles aren't all that new.

So, what is it that is new? It's mainly the use of adaptive systems in IT development and the name "Agile" that are new. In the old days, IT development projects were very different and required a precise, predictive method. Later on, as computers evolved, the nature of those projects and their audiences changed. In most cases, predictive systems weren't a great choice anymore, but practitioners continued using them. That was the case until a group of people involved in those projects started reinventing the adaptive method.

2. Scrum

Agile is the concept of using of an **adaptive approach**. This is a high-level, abstract concept, and we need a practical approach to run projects based on this concept. That's where the methodologies (and frameworks) come into play.

There are a few first-generation Agile methods/frameworks, among which Scrum is the most popular nowadays. Scrum has dominated the market so much that people have a hard time talking about Agile without making it specific to Scrum.

Besides the first-generation methods, there are also new ones available, which are usually inspired and influenced by Scrum, and generally have the goal of scaling Scrum for larger projects.

The core framework of Scrum is described in the **Scrum Guide** by Ken Schwaber and Jeff Sutherland (https://scrumguides.org). It's a guide that's generally accepted as the official definition of Scrum – although, it's important to note that many great experts have contributed to Scrum, and it wouldn't be what we know today if it wasn't for them.

2.1 Scrum as a Framework

Most Scrum practitioners are very sensitive about the word "methodology" and prefer to call Scrum a framework instead. It's difficult to explain the exact difference between the two because there's no clear distinction, but the overall idea is that a methodology is more sophisticated, supports complicated situations, and needs to be simplified if you want to use it for simpler projects, whereas a framework is the bare minimum needed in all projects, and needs to be expanded to support more complicated projects. Sometimes, methodologies are said to be prescriptive, and frameworks are said to be descriptive.

In reality, the difference between a methodology and a framework is a matter of degree rather than substance, and the fear of using the word "methodology" seems to have its roots in bad experiences that some practitioners have had with methodologies in the past.

2.2 Scrum as a Wrapper

Unlike other systems such as eXtreme Programming, Scrum doesn't provide practices, techniques, and tools. It's just a simple framework of management activities that can serve as a wrapper for other processes, practices, and techniques. Some people believe that Scrum was originally created to provide a management layer for eXtreme Programming.

Regardless, what you get from Scrum is just that: a simple wrapper within which you have to add the practices and techniques that are suitable for your project. It helps you organize them via the management layer it adds to the project.

2.3 The Scrum Structure

Each Scrum project is done in a number of **Sprints**. "Sprint" is the Scrum term for "iteration".

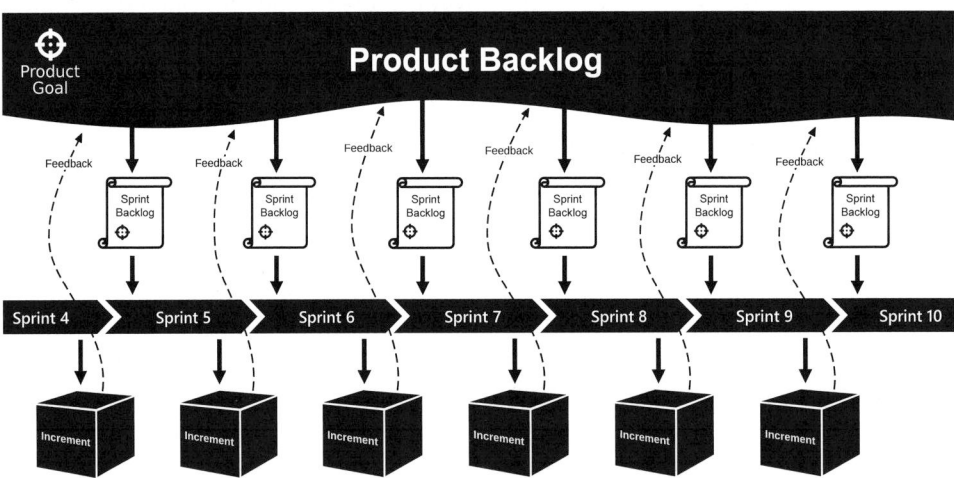

We use a **Product Backlog** to store the remaining work items. When it's time to start a new Sprint, we pick a number of items from the top of the Product Backlog and add them to the **Sprint Backlog**, which is our plan for the upcoming Sprint. We run Sprints as many times as required until either everything is done or the customer decides that the existing features are enough and the remaining low-value ones can be ignored.

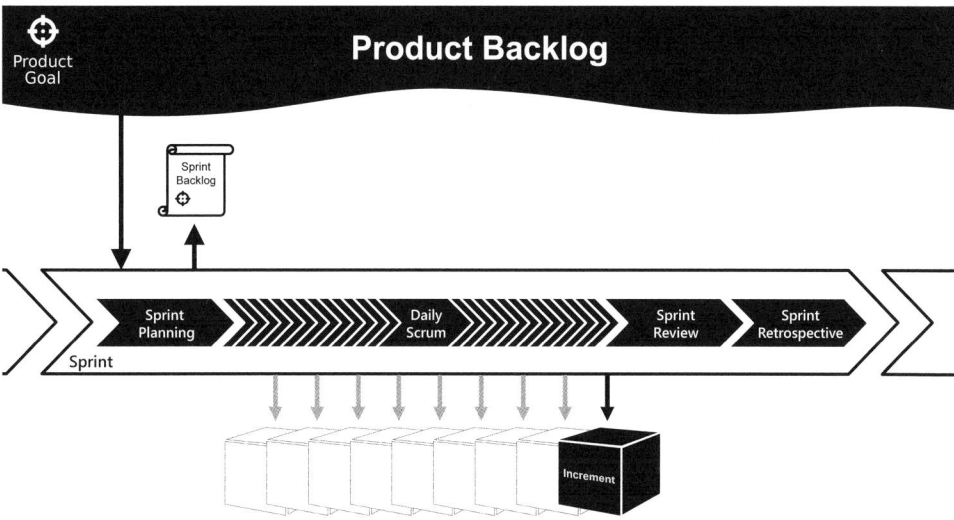

Each Sprint is a container for a number of events:
- **Sprint Planning:** for planning of the upcoming Sprint by creating a Sprint Backlog
- **Daily Scrum:** a 15-minute daily meeting for synchronization
- **Sprint Review:** for reviewing the latest increment and progress information, and receiving feedback
- **Sprint Retrospective:** for reviewing the way of working and for planning for improvements for the next Sprint

Finally, there are three roles in Scrum:
- **Product Owner:** This person is responsible for maximizing the value of the product and achieving the Product Goal, which is mainly achieved by creating and maintaining the Product Backlog.
- **Scrum Master:** This person ensures that the Scrum framework is followed entirely and correctly, which requires coaching, training, and problem solving.
- **Developers:** This is the group of technical experts who develop the product.

In the rest of this chapter, we'll review these aspects in more detail.

2.3.1 People
There are many people who have an interest in the project and can impact it, such as the Scrum Team, the other people in the supplier organization, the customer, the end-users, and even sometimes regulators and competitors. In project management, all these people are called **stakeholders**, and the idea is that we must identify all of them and understand their requirements. For example, some projects only focus on

the customer requirements and overlook the requirements dictated by the regulators, which may cause serious problems in the future.

Agile systems don't have special considerations for the wide range of stakeholders, mainly because this is not as sensitive in IT development as it is in some other types of project. However, it's still helpful if you do pay attention. Another consequence is that Agile systems in general, and Scrum in particular, use the word "stakeholder" to refer to the customer, or the customer and the end-users. So, if you have a background and knowledge in project management, you should consider this terminology when reading resources about Scrum.

For now, let's focus on the people internal to the project: the **Scrum Team**. We'll check the important attributes of the team as a whole, and then the details of each role inside the team.

2.3.1.1 Attributes
Let's review some of the Scrum Team attributes and rules before going into the details of the three roles.

Size
As you will see in the following sections, the Scrum Team is a flat organization without a centralized coordination system. As a result, it can't work if the team is too big. Normally, there are 10 or fewer people in the Scrum Team.

For larger projects that need more people, they can work in multiple teams. A setup with multiple teams is called **Scaled Scrum**, which will be discussed at the end of this chapter.

Some people think that adding more Developers would increase the development speed. This may or may not be the case, and even when it is, the impact is not linear. A classical form of this issue is what **Brooks' law** states: "Adding manpower to a late software project makes it later.", and alternatively, "Nine women can't make a baby in one month."

Part-time or full-time
We always prefer to have team members who work full-time on the project because they won't be distracted by other responsibilities. However, this is not always possible, and we may have to compromise, so all three roles can be either full-time or part-time as necessary.

Having multiple roles
Scrum Team members usually have only one of the three roles. However, it's possible for a single person to take on multiple roles, if it's really needed. This is usually a

consideration in teams and organizations that are too small; otherwise, if a person has extra time as a Product Owner or a Scrum Master, they can become the Product Owner or Scrum Master in multiple projects, instead of taking on a Developer role in the same project.

When taking on multiple roles, the person obviously needs to have the necessary expertise for both roles on the one hand, while on the other hand making sure that neither role is eclipsing the others. For example, if a person is both a Product Owner and a Developer, they have to make sure that when they are attending the Daily Scrum, they are doing it as a Developer, and not as a Product Owner, because Daily Scrums are only for Developers.

Cross-functionality
We don't want the team to be dependent on external people, and therefore, we want to have cross-functional teams that have all the expertise required for the product. We do that by composing a team that covers all types of expertise. Note that it is the team as a whole that needs to be cross-functional, not each and every individual inside the team.

Sometimes, you need a special skill for a limited period, and in most projects, that work will be referred to an expert outside the team. In Scrum, to keep the team cross-functional, when such a person is needed, we bring them inside the team (usually as a part-time member) for one or a few Sprints. The difference in this scenario is that the person with the specialist expertise must see themselves as one of the members of the team, and follow the same rules and processes as the rest.

Self-management
A Scrum Team needs to have the authority to make decisions about the project. In the previous versions of the Scrum Guide, this used to be called **self-organization**, whereas in the 2020 version it is called **self-management**. These are simply two different terms for the same concept.

The reason we want the project decisions to be made inside the team is that it helps increase their productivity, as otherwise, they would have to escalate issues to higher levels of management and wait for them to respond.

Empowerment of the teams is never absolute for various reasons:
- They still have to follow the Scrum framework; for example, they do not have the authority to remove the Sprint Retrospectives.
- They should follow the organizational standards and rules; for example, they should follow the same coding standard as for every other project.
- While Scrum says that they make all the project decisions, there are still decisions that belong to the customer, as the ultimate owner of the product, that no one else can make on their behalf.

Levels of commitment
A pig and a chicken are hanging out, and the chicken suggests they open a restaurant. "What should we serve?" the pig asks enthusiastically. The chicken replies, "Ham and eggs". The pig rejects the idea (not surprisingly), saying, "I would be committed, while you would be only involved".

The whole Scrum Team are the pigs in this analogy, while the rest of the stakeholders, including the customer and senior management, are just chickens.

In line with this analogy, it was common in the early days of Agile to refer to various project stakeholders as chickens and pigs, according to their levels of commitment, and then give them different treatments based on that. For example, different people may be present in a Sprint Planning meeting, but only the Scrum Team members are pigs and the rest are chickens. The pigs are allowed to talk while the rest can only observe.

This analogy and terminology is not used so commonly anymore, but the concept remains valid.

Changing the team composition
We prefer to have stable teams that stay fixed during the project. However, if it's required to add or remove a few team members, it's best not to do it in the middle of the Sprint because it's distracting.

2.3.1.2 Roles
Now that we're done reviewing the attributes of the Scrum Team, let's review the roles inside the team.

There are three roles inside the team, each of which has defined accountabilities and responsibilities. Like any other system, it's possible to delegate the responsibilities to someone else inside the team, but the original role stays accountable.

To explain the difference between responsibility and accountability in simple words, you're "responsible" for something when you're supposed to do it; whereas you're "accountable" for something when you have to answer for its results. This means that when you're accountable but prefer to transfer the responsibility, you probably still supervise the work to make sure it's done properly.

The Product Owner
Most projects have multiple people from the business or customer side who have a say in the requirements. It's distracting and difficult for the Developers to be in touch with them and use their input to prioritize their work because there are usually a lot of inconsistencies among their inputs. The common solution for this issue is to have one person or a group of people as the central hub. All the business inputs go into this hub, the inconsistencies are resolved, and a clear set of prioritized requirements are prepared for the Developers. Scrum's Product Owner is that central hub.

In order to be able to work with business-oriented people (external or internal customer), the Product Owner has to be business-oriented as well, and also have an understanding of the vision and goals of the product. They use this information to manage the Product Backlog by:
- composing new items for the backlog,
- detailing the existing items, and
- ordering the items.

To achieve the highest possible value as soon as possible, the items are ordered in such a way that those that have the most potential for contributing to the value of the product will be at the top of the backlog and will be developed first. This is one major way in which the Product Owner maximizes value.

– Affiliation
When the project is done for an external customer, some people call the customer's representative the Product Owner. In most cases, though, it's not a good idea, and you need to have someone from your organization to take on this role.

– Number of Product Owners
This role belongs to one person, no matter how large the project is. This is so, because if there's more than one person, they may cause inconsistencies in the Product Backlog and in the information provided to the Developers.

There can be a committee for product ownership, but even in such a case, there should be one person representing this committee, and this one person should be called the Product Owner. In this way, at least the Developers won't be confused by receiving information from multiple people.

- Communications
While it's not forbidden for Developers to have direct communication with the external stakeholders, most of the communications are done by or enabled by the Product Owner. The Product Owner is constantly in touch with the customer and end-user representatives and makes sure that all feedback is reflected in the Product backlog.

Besides the external communications, Product Owners also have a lot to do with internal communications. After all, they are responsible for the requirements, and they need to make sure that everyone understands them correctly, and that what the Developers do really satisfy the needs of the customer and end-user. As a result, whenever the Developers have a doubt about some functionality, the Product Owner is the one who clarifies it for them.

- Progress measurement
The Product Owner is responsible for measuring the progress of the project. This is their responsibility because it requires a high-level understanding of the whole scope of the work and all the possibilities related to it, and no one has more information about this area than the Product Owner. The Developers are focused on the work of the Sprints and the technical aspects of the project, while the Scrum Master is focused on the context rather than the content.

When it comes to progress measurement, the most important measurement in most projects is the completion date, and that's the main thing the Product Owner does in a Scrum project as well.

Finally, the Product Owner makes sure that all the information on progress is transparent and available to the relevant stakeholders.

- Ownership
The Product Owner **owns** the Product Backlog, which means that they are accountable for the Product Backlog, and no one is allowed to make changes to it other than the Product Owner, or possibly people who are authorized by the Product Owner when some responsibilities have been delegated to them.

No one is allowed to override the decisions of the Product Owner (e.g., the order of items), but it doesn't mean that they can't influence these decisions. Indeed, the Product Owner's decisions can be considerably influenced by the business decisions of the customer and the technical input of the Developers.

– Delegation
Product Owners are allowed to delegate some of their responsibilities to others (usually the Developers). For example, it's not uncommon for the Product Owner to ask the Developers to take responsibility for creating the technical items in the Product Backlog. However, in general, it's best if the Product Owner is active enough and keeps the responsibilities to themselves.

The Scrum Master
Scrum Masters are Scrum experts who help everyone understand and use Scrum. They also help create a smooth working environment for the team.

– Coaching and training
The Scrum Master coaches and trains the team in using Scrum, and more importantly, may need to teach and coach the customer and the management layers of the organization how to work with the Scrum Team.

– The watchdog
The Scrum Master should make sure that the Scrum framework is used properly, and if not, take action to correct it. For example, some people think that they don't need to have Sprint Retrospectives because they are mature enough. In a case like this, the Scrum Master has to explain to them why they always need this meeting, and find a way to convince them to do the right thing.

Remember that the Scrum Master can't order the team members to do certain things – they can only convince them.

– Impediments
When there's an impediment to the work of the team members, the members should try to solve it themselves, but if they don't know how to do it or it's too difficult for them to solve on their own, the Scrum Master will take on the responsibility.

In the past, the Scrum Master used to be introduced as the one who removes impediments, but it's been replaced in the newer versions of the Scrum Guide by "the one who causes the removal of impediments", to ensure that the availability of their help doesn't block the self-organization of the team.

– Facilitation
Facilitation is key in projects. Although, the default Scrum setup with 10 or fewer team members and a few customer and end-user representatives is not the biggest facilitation challenge in the world, the availability of an expert facilitator still helps, and this role is taken by the Scrum Master.

Similar to what was said about the removal of impediments, facilitation is not done by default because it may block the self-organization of the team. The Scrum Master facilitates only when requested or required to do so.

– *Techniques*
Working in an adaptive environment has its own challenges. For example, as a Developer, how would you manage the database without an upfront design?

Whenever the Developers or the Product Owner have problems with techniques, tools, and practices, it's the Scrum Master who helps them find the appropriate ones. This means that a proper Scrum Master needs to have technical information as well, which makes it a difficult role.

Note that what is said here doesn't mean that the Scrum Master works as a proxy. They don't do this because it blocks the self-organization of the team. Instead of doing the work for the other team members, they teach them how to do those things.

– *The organization*
The people who play the role of Scrum Master for the projects of an organization are the ones who help the organization adapt itself to this way of working and implement Scrum in its projects. In addition, a Scrum Master may be in touch with the higher levels of the organization to win support and resources for the team.

– *Content vs. context*
The Scrum Master is focused on the context (the framework, processes, practices, techniques, relationships, etc.) rather than on the content (items on the Product Backlog, features in the Increments, etc.).

This is an important distinction, and a framing that helps you understand what should or shouldn't be done by the Scrum Master. For example, is it a good idea for the Scrum Master to be responsible for measuring the progress of the project? The answer is no, because we need to inspect the content of the project in order to measure its progress.

– *A management position*
Scrum Master is a management position. However, it's about managing the process rather than the people. Indeed, this may not be enough to call this role a management role, but it's a remainder of the early days of Scrum, when they invented this role to replace the other management roles involved in the project.

A common issue in many Scrum projects is that the Scrum Masters practically manage the teams; for example, they assign work to the Developers. This is not correct, because the Developers are self-managing and capable of doing it by themselves (in fact, they know better than anyone else how to do it), and furthermore, the Scrum Master has to be focused on the context.

The Developers
Developers are application area experts who are responsible for delivering backlog items and managing their own efforts.

Many people use the word "developer" to refer to programmers, but in the Agile context, the word "developer" usually refers to anyone who helps build the product. These may be experts in programming, testing, analysis, architecture, UI design etc.

- Shared accountability
All Developers share accountability for the development of the product. This means that one or a few Developers may create a particular feature, but all Developers stay accountable for that feature, and if something goes wrong in the future, no one is allowed to say "This wasn't my fault." (Of course, the Scrum Master should try to create an environment in which people don't blame each other anyway.)

Another aspect of sharing accountability is that no one owns any part of the code, and no one is allowed to say, "This is my module, don't touch it without me."

- Titles
The Developers shouldn't have any titles; for example, there are no "testers" in Scrum (because that's a title), but there are Developers who are expert in testing. This seemingly small detail is important because if you call someone a "tester", that person will feel more responsible for testing and less responsible for other aspects of the work. While we don't force people to do something they're not expert in, we still want them to share accountability and collaborate, and making the titles forbidden helps with this.

- Cross-functionality
As mentioned before, only the team as a whole is cross-functional and not the individuals inside the team. Some Developers are expert in programming, some in testing, some in designing, and so on. When they get together, they form a team that has all the expertise and can indeed be called cross-functional.

Although individual Developers are not expected to have all the skills needed for the product, a common pattern that forms in highly collaborative environments is that people start to learn the general aspects of all skills besides their own specialist area in which they have full expertise. This is called a **T-shaped skill set**, and it works very well in Agile.

The last thing we may need to review is the scope of cross-functionality. Most of the Scrum resources, including the Scrum Guide, mix two different scopes of cross-functionality when they refer to this concept. One is the set of skills needed to exist among the Developers to build a certain set of features for the product, and the other scope is wider and contains the managerial support needed for the product, and from that perspective, it's the Developers along with the Product Owner and Scrum Master who become truly cross-functional.

2.3.1.3 Extra roles

According to Scrum, it's not permitted to have additional roles. Team leader, project manager, and all other possible roles are not welcome in a Scrum Team. This is so because the accountabilities and responsibilities required for a small Scrum project are already defined in the framework, and there's no overlooked responsibility that may require a new role (at least according to Scrum).

On the other hand, in the case of roles such as project manager, it may not be compatible with the nature of a Scrum project because the project manager role is a centralized coordination and facilitation system, while Scrum uses a distributed form of it, and each of the three Scrum roles has a few project management responsibilities.

Note that what is said here about the project manager role only applies to Scrum, and not to Agile in general. There are well-formed Agile methods that have a project manager role, or at least don't have a problem with having such a role.

2.3.2 Events

Next, we're going to review the five Scrum events. These meetings are enough for most of our needs, which means that they reduce the need for time-consuming ad hoc meetings. In other words, they instill regularity into the project and give it a constant pace.

All events are **timeboxed**, meaning that they have a limited time, and therefore, people have to be focused on the goals and the important tasks without spending time on the fancy aspects of the work.

In each event, one or a few things will be inspected, and based on the results, we will adapt. Remember that adaptation is key in Agile projects.

2.3.2.1 Sprint

Each Scrum project delivers the product in a number of iterations called Sprints. Instead of having a continuous flow of work based on a huge Product Backlog, we break it down into Sprints, and in each Sprint we will focus on a small Sprint Backlog. This is a common technique that helps reduce distractions and increase productivity.

The Sprint is one of the five events in Scrum, but it's different from the rest in that it's a container for the other four events.

Duration of Sprints
Sprints should be 1 month or shorter.

Scrum uses the same duration for all Sprints to make it simpler and more regular. So, the whole Scrum Team decides about the suitable timeboxed duration of Sprints, sets it, and uses that for all Sprints. It means that we don't decide about the duration of Sprints every time we want to start a new one, but there's nothing stopping us from revising this duration if we change our mind as we learn more about the project. If a revision is needed, it's best to discuss it in the Sprint Retrospective meeting, and make the change effective in the next Sprint. You shouldn't change the duration in the middle of a Sprint.

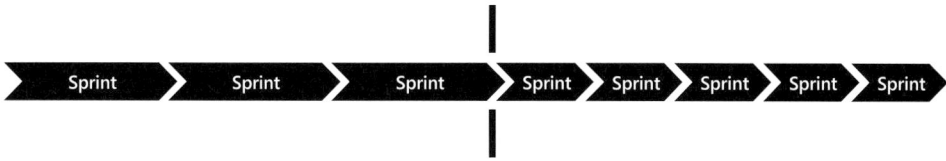

When Sprints are shorter, there are more feedback loops, and in particular, more Sprint Review meetings. This helps reduce risks and increase adaptation. However, on the other hand, each Sprint has its own overhead of meetings, and if Sprints are too short, there won't be enough development for a meaningful Sprint Review. It follows that, the optimum timeboxed duration of Sprints depends on your project.

A plan for the Sprint
The Sprint Backlog is the plan for the Sprint. It contains a number of items from the Product Backlog, and the tasks you create by decomposing those items. Another element in this plan is the Sprint Goal, which is a step toward the high-level Product Goal, and gives direction to the otherwise random activities inside the Sprint.

Cancelling Sprints

While you're working, something significant may change in the project environment that makes the plans for the Sprint obsolete (especially the Sprint Goal). In this case, instead of revising the whole plan, the Product Owner has the authority to cancel the Sprint, and then a new Sprint with a new plan will start.

It's not common to have a lot of cancelled Sprints because we can't expect many significant changes in the short duration of a single Sprint.

Some people think that they must deliver all or at least most of the items in the Sprint Backlog, and that if they realize that it's not possible to deliver all of them, they have to cancel the Sprint. This is not true, though. We are not committed to delivering all the items in the Sprint Backlog, but our commitment is to move toward the Sprint Goal and do our best. At the end of the Sprint, we will simply deliver the items that are done and return the rest to the Product Backlog.

Stability

The main reason we need to have Sprints is to reduce distractions. It increases focus when we use a small Sprint Backlog instead of a huge Product Backlog, and also when we keep some sensitive things fixed during the Sprint. Typically, the following are fixed for the duration of the Sprint:
- The timeboxed duration of the Sprint;
- The minimum level of quality;
- The composition of the team;
- The Sprint Goal.

Traditionally, the Product Backlog items in the Sprint Backlog used to be fixed as well, because changing them is the most important source of distraction. Based on the Scrum Guide, this approach is not mandatory to increase flexibility, especially in comparison with iteration-free Kanban systems that are considered by some people to be more modern and more adaptive. However, the other side of the coin is that allowing changes to the Sprint Backlog items violates one of the main purposes of having Sprints and Sprint Backlogs.

No Sprint Zero

Some people have a special Sprint at the beginning of the project to prepare the environment, and they call it Sprint Zero. This is not a good idea because even the preparation should be adaptive and gradual, based on what emerges throughout the project, rather than being upfront.

There's no Sprint Zero, and all Sprints are the same, in that you create new Increments of the product in them.

No complementary Sprints

Some people have special Sprints for tying up loose ends and prepare the Increment for release. This is totally unacceptable because each item you work on during the Sprint must be absolutely done before you consider it as part of the Increment, and all Increments must be releasable. It's important that we have done items and releasable Increments because that makes the Increments more representative and generates more reliable feedback. On the other hand, it makes the whole project more predictable; otherwise, you never know how much trouble you'll have to go through to truly finish them (which is, by the way, much more time consuming when not done immediately).

There's no Integration Sprint, Hardening Sprint, Release Sprint, and so on. All Sprints are the same, and they all create releasable Increments containing 100% done items.

2.3.2.2 Sprint Planning

All projects need planning, including Agile ones. The Sprint Planning meeting is a planning activity in Scrum, but not the only one. It's the first thing done in a Sprint when the Scrum Team members get together and plan it.

The results of this planning activity are stored in a Sprint Backlog. More details will be added to this plan during the Sprint.

Duration

The Sprint Planning meeting is timeboxed and lasts a maximum of 8 hours. If the Sprint is shorter than 1 month, it's normal to have shorter Sprint Planning meetings.

Most early resources about Scrum used to suggest a duration proportional to the duration of Sprints; i.e., 4-hour Sprint Planning meetings if Sprints are 2 weeks long. This has been removed from the Scrum Guide to make it more flexible, but the proportional approach still seems reasonable.

The whole Scrum Team decides about the timeboxed duration of Sprint Planning meetings, and similarly to what was said about the duration of Sprints, it will be used for all Sprint Planning meetings, unless you decide to revise it in the future.

Topics
Three topics, around the **why**, **what**, and **how** questions should be discussed in the Sprint Planning meeting. Let's review them next.

– *Why?*
Why are you going to have this Sprint?

The answer would be your next **Sprint Goal**. This goal has to be aligned with the **Product Goal**, which is the overall objective of the project.

Whenever you have doubts about items, you can interpret them based on the Sprint Goal. In this sense, it directs your activities. It's useful to have a goal and not be limited to isolated activities or features.

The whole Scrum Team together composes the Sprint Goal.

– *What?*
After preparing the Sprint Goal, the team makes their plan more concrete by selecting a number of items from the Product Backlog and moving them to the Sprint Backlog. These will be the features, bug fixes, etc. that they will complete during the Sprint.

In its early days, Scrum used to be all about maximizing value, but the 2020 version of the Scrum Guide has paid a lot of attention to the goals (the Product Goal and the Scrum Goal), which is closer to the common approach in established project management methods. As a result, there's a small contradiction in the process at this moment. On one hand, there's the notion of ordering the items in the Product Backlog in a way that maximizes value, and therefore, items for the Sprint Backlog would be picked from the top of the Product Backlog; while on the other hand, we have this need to align the items we pick with a certain goal. We can imagine that the Product Owner dynamically changes the order of the items in such a way that those on top of the Product Backlog are the most valuable among those that are compatible with the Sprint Goal, and then the Developers pick those items.

Product Backlog

Regardless of the issue above, composing the Sprint Goal and selecting the items for the Sprint Backlog have to be done iteratively, meaning that you will compose the Sprint Backlog and start picking the items, and then based on the items you have picked you may adjust the Sprint Goal, and then based on the adjusted Sprint Goal you may want to switch some of the items, and so on.

One common issue in Sprint Planning is the number of items picked for the Sprint. It's up to the Developers, and no one else, to decide how many items they want to pick. Forcing the Developers to pick more items can have multiple counterproductive consequences.

While selecting the items, the Product Owner probably explains every item to make sure that the Developers have the correct understanding of them and that there will be no surprises later on.

– *How?*
Finally, when you have the Sprint Goal and you have selected the items for the Sprint, it's time for the Developers to think about those items and see how they want to build them. The result is a number of tasks (usually technical). In other words, they will break down the items into tasks.

As usual, we don't need to have a complete upfront plan. The Developers don't need to break down all the items – doing it for the first few items suffices, and the rest can be done during the Sprint.

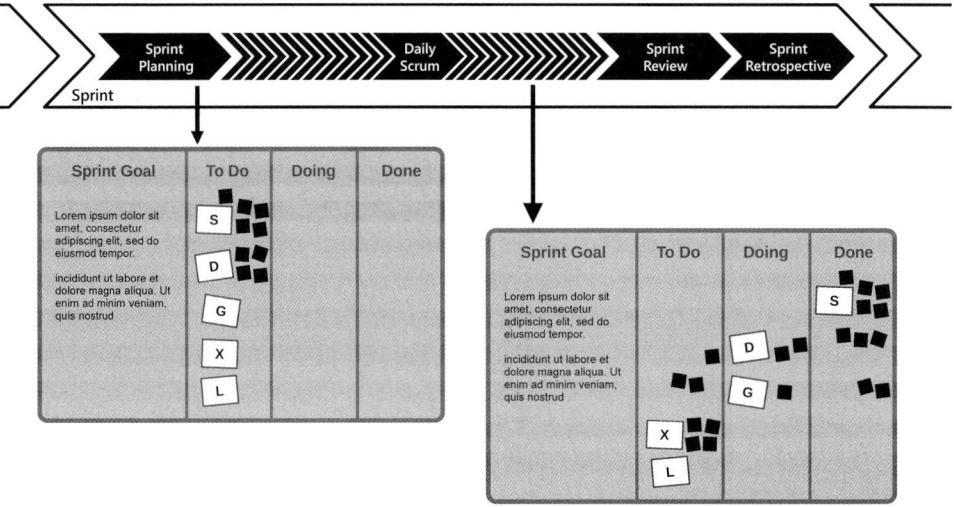

The results of working on the three topics of Sprint Planning (the Sprint Goal, Product Backlog items, and tasks), will be captured in the Sprint Backlog.

Readiness

Most items are initially large and unclear in the Product Backlog. When they move to the top of the Product Backlog, we break them down into smaller items and spend more time making them clearer.

We want the items on the top of the Product Backlog to have the following characteristics:
- Small enough to be done in one Sprint;
- Clear enough and with some form of implicit or explicit acceptance criteria.

Such items are **ready** to be developed in the Sprint. However, what happens if the items on the top of the Product Backlog are not ready?

In this case, we don't skip them because they're not ready, but we go on and pick them for the Sprint. During the Sprint, we will refine them by adding more detail to them. This is so because we don't want readiness to be a gate for starting to work on an item, but rather, we want to be focused on the most valuable items first.

Some people create a **Definition of Ready**. This is usually unnecessary because:
- the readiness concept is simple and doesn't need a per-project elaboration in a concept like a "definition of ready", and
- when there is such a definition, chances are the team will use it as a gate for starting the development of items, which is not a good idea.

2.3.2.3 Daily Scrum

Regardless of the development approach, it's a good idea to have short daily meetings for the project to let everyone know what's going on. This is even more important in adaptive environments because they don't have detailed upfront plans.

Duration
The Daily Scrum is normally 15 minutes long. One common trick is to hold it standing up (its generic name is the "daily stand-up") because it helps keep it short.

Regularity
We prefer to hold the Daily Scrum meetings at the same time and place. Otherwise, some time has to be spent every day arranging for the next meeting, which is not justifiable.

It's common for Developers to hold this meeting in front of their Sprint Backlog, which is usually a large board on the wall. Some teams prefer to hold it at the beginning of each day, and some at the end of each day. Some teams even prefer to do it in the middle of the day, when they are sure everyone is present.

Difficulties arise when there's a **virtual team** with people from different time zones. Compromises have to be made in setting the time of the meeting for such teams, and video conferencing can help create an environment similar to face-to-face meetings. Despite that, when possible, we prefer to have **co-located** teams with **face-to-face communications**.

Attendance
The Daily Scrum meeting is only for the Developers. Anyone else (Product Owner, Scrum Master, managers, customer, team members from other projects, etc.) can attend the meeting, but they need to be quiet and only observe.

Purpose
The purpose of this meeting is to let the Developers know what's happening in the project, and to synchronize them. They will inspect their progress, which can be called **progress toward the Sprint Goal**, and think about or plan their work for the next 24 hours. They usually update the Sprint Backlog during the meeting, although it is not limited to this meeting.

To make sure that the meeting is regular and all Developers contribute, it's a tradition to go one person at a time, answering three questions:
1. What have you completed since the last meeting?
2. What do you plan to complete by the next meeting?
3. What is getting in your way?

While this is very common in Agile projects and was implied as mandatory in the earlier versions of the Scrum Guide, they later removed it because they believe that there can be more than one way of managing this meeting and it has to be up to the Developers to see what's best. Still, going through the three standard questions seems to be the best choice.

Managing issues
No matter how the Daily Scrum meeting is conducted (with or without going through the three questions), the obstacles have to be mentioned. However, this meeting is only about identifying and communicating the obstacles and not solving them, because solving them may require a lot of time.

If a Developer says that they have a difficulty and you know how to solve it, you should wait for the meeting to end, and then try to help that Developer.

Not a status meeting
Some teams use the Daily Scrum as a status meeting for reporting their performance to the Product Owner, Scrum Master, or someone else. This is not its main purpose, though, and they need to be focused on synchronizing and planning instead. Remember that the Daily Scrum is a meeting for the Developers.

In general, we prefer to have a large Sprint Backlog on the wall, where anyone can come and see our Sprint progress, and in addition to that, review the progress of the project in the Sprint Review meeting. These forms of progress reporting should be enough for a typical project.

Monitoring Sprint progress
One of the topics in the Daily Scrum meeting is inspecting progress toward the Sprint Goal, which is, to put it simply, the progress of the Sprint. It's up to the Developers to decide how to do that. Measuring progress toward a goal that is not quantified is not easy, and always subjective. However, it's common for teams to measure the amount of remaining work across time, and they may also draw a **burn-down chart** for it.

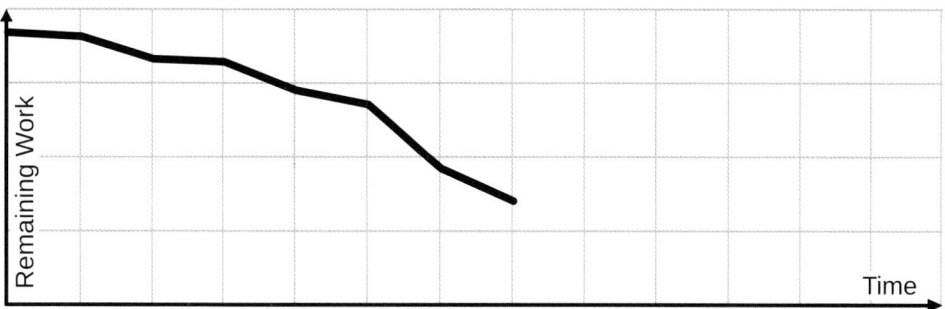

Using burn-down charts is optional in Scrum. They can be used for visualizing the progress of Sprints and the progress of the whole project. We'll talk more about them in the Crystal chapter.

2.3.2.4 Sprint Review

We set a small goal for each Sprint and focus on achieving that goal. At the end of the Sprint, we have a review meeting to go through everything with the customer and receive feedback, which is crucial for our adaptive approach.

Duration
The Sprint Review meeting is a maximum of 4 hours in a 1-month Sprint, and usually shorter when Sprints are shorter. It's timeboxed, and as usual, we set its timeboxed duration once and use that for all instances of the meeting, unless we decide to revise it based on what we've learned from the project.

Regularity
If possible, it would be advantageous to hold the meeting at the same time and place every time. For example, it can be on the last working day of each month when the Sprints are 1 month long and start at the beginning of each month.

This is helpful because everything becomes more regular and the customer and end-user representatives can match their other engagements with us and attend the meetings more easily.

Attendance

The whole Scrum Team, the customer, and possibly end-user representatives and advisers will attend this meeting and participate in reviewing the Sprint and giving feedback.

Topics

We go through several topics in this meeting:
- We review the last Increment and let the customer and end-user representatives work with it and give us feedback. This is probably the most important part of this meeting because of our need for adaptation.
- The Product Owner informs everyone of the progress of the project.
- Everyone discusses what to do next.

The Product Owner uses the feedback generated in this meeting to revise the Product Backlog.

Monitoring project performance

Both the customer and the performing organization need to have an idea of when the project will be finished: for the customer to arrange it with its business operations, and for the performing organization to plan for the next projects. As a result, communicating the progress of the project is one of the topics for the Sprint Review meeting.

Progress measurement for the whole project is done by the Product Owner, because they have the best understanding of the range of items in the Product Backlog and the possibilities for the future. Just a reminder: It's the Developers who measure the progress of Sprints.

The progress of the project is measured toward its **Product Goal**. It's up to the Product Owner to decide which parameters to use and how to calculate them, but one of the best ways is to forecast when the goal will be achieved. The Product Owner usually does it by considering the existing items in the Product Backlog, as well as what they guess will be added to the backlog in the future on the one hand, and the rate of development (velocity) on the other.

Similarly to the Sprint progress, it's common, but not mandatory, to use a burn-down chart to visualize the progress of the project.

2.3.2.5 Sprint Retrospective

Adaptive systems are about adapting the product to its environment, and the Sprint Review meeting is one of the main events for doing so. However, we also need to adapt our way of working to suit the environment. The latter is not limited to adaptive projects, and it's always necessary. However, Agile projects take this more seriously, and usually have reflective meetings at the end of their iterations dedicated to improving the way we work. This meeting is called Sprint Retrospective in Scrum.

The Sprint Retrospective is a structured way of improving our process, but we see it as a minimum, and we don't limit our improvements to the Sprint Retrospective meetings. Improvements can happen at any time.

Duration
The Sprint Retrospective takes a maximum of 3 hours in a 1-month Sprint, and usually less in shorter Sprints. As usual, it's timeboxed, and its timeboxed duration is set for all instances of the meeting, which are kept the same unless we decide to revise them.

Attendance
All Scrum Team members participate in this meeting and collaborate to find a way to improve the next Sprint.

Scope
This meeting is about the process and not the product; it's about the context and not the content. For example, you may talk about the way the Product Backlog is refined, but you won't refine the Product Backlog; you may talk about the range and method of testing the product, but you won't test the product; etc.

Output
The output of this meeting is one or a few improvements planned for the way we work in the next Sprint.

Some people think that their team is mature enough, and therefore, no longer needs Sprint Retrospectives. This is not realistic, and it's hard to imagine a team so perfect that they can't make any improvements at all.

A common problem in making any improvement is to aim too high, have too many improvements planned, or have improvements that are too complicated. It's best to limit it to just one realistic improvement: the one that seems to be the most important.

Managing the plans
A new statement was added to the 2017 edition of the Scrum Guide, stating that in this meeting at least one improvement plan will be designed, and it will be added to the next Sprint Backlog. Unfortunately, this introduces two problems:

1. It mixes the items related to the product with items related to the process. Normally, we expect the Product Backlog and the Sprint Backlogs to be about the product, and nothing else.
2. We normally like to say that everything in the Sprint Backlog originates from the Product Backlog because we want to make sure that items are compatible with each other and prioritized properly, and that we're not only responding to what seems to be the most urgent work. However, the statement above adds something to the Sprint Backlog that doesn't originate from the Product Backlog, and so breaks the rule.

The 2020 edition of the Scrum Guide changed that part, and now it doesn't say that you should do it, but that you can if you want to. Despite that, it still assumes that everything in the Sprint Backlog originates from the Product Backlog.

2.3.3 Artifacts
So far, we've reviewed the roles and the events. The next Scrum concept is artifacts.

There are three artifacts in Scrum:
- **Increment** is the latest version of the product we've created for the customer.
- **Product Backlog** is our overall plan for the project, containing the Product Goal, and an ordered list of the items (such as features) we may add to the product.
- **Sprint Backlog** is our short-term plan for the project that will be implemented in a single Sprint. It contains the Sprint Goal, a list of Product Backlog items we've selected for the Sprint, and a number of tasks we've created by decomposing the items.

There's a **commitment** for each artifact, which is used to interpret that artifact and direct the efforts:
- **Definition of Done** is the commitment for the Increment that makes it clear what we mean when we say something is done.
- **Product Goal** is the commitment for the Product Backlog that makes it clear what we want to achieve by developing the items. It's our vision for the product, or derived from our vision for the product.
- **Sprint Goal** is the commitment for the Sprint Backlog that makes it clear what we want to achieve in the Sprint by developing the Product Backlog items in the Sprint Backlog. Each Sprint has its own Sprint Backlog and Sprint Goal.

2.3.3.1 Product Backlog
The Product Backlog is our overall plan for the project and product – our understanding of what is expected from the product. It's where we reflect on all the feedback, resolve conflicting requirements, and set priorities. It's where all the work for the Sprints originates.

The Product Backlog may be stored in an application or a digital file, but we prefer it to be a low-tech board on the wall in our project room.

It contains the following:
- The Product Goal;
- The items (ordered based on their importance).

Product Goal
The Product Goal is our vision for the product or at least an intermediate step toward a high-level vision. It's what we want to achieve by developing the items. It's useful to have such a goal and be focused on that to give direction to our efforts instead of just working on random items.

In the past, Scrum was only focused on "generating value", and while there was an unofficial idea of having an optional "product vision", it was never an embedded, serious element. The 2020 version of the Scrum Guide has followed the path of established project management systems and added the concept of the Product Goal, which is very helpful, although the idea of maximizing value still exists in a standalone way and sometimes conflicts with the new concept of the Product Goal. More time is probably needed in this community to observe this new concept and truly embed it into the framework.

There's only one Product Goal at any point in time, but after a while, this goal may be met (or canceled) and replaced with a new goal. When seen from the perspective of most systems, this is like having multiple projects run one after the other, each with a different goal for the same product. Scrum, on the other hand, keeps all of these efforts under the same umbrella without trying to package them as separate projects. This probably has roots in the fact that some Agile practitioners are not so comfortable with what they know as "projects" and prefer to only think about "products" instead, which is not correct, as projects are simply structured ways of thinking about products.

Completeness
Some teams think that trying to create a complete Product Backlog before starting the development is a good idea. However, as you already know, this goes against the idea of having an adaptive project. We need to accept the fact that we never know exactly what is needed for the product and we should go on with an incomplete backlog and create Increments to understand our environment better, and decide about the next steps. If we do know everything about the project upfront, it's better to use a predictive approach instead.

The Product Backlog can never be considered complete, as it's a dynamic, changing artifact that emerges throughout the project.

Based on what has been said, the way we start the project is more or less clear: We spend only a few days on composing the Product Goal and creating enough items for the first one (or few) Sprints, and then immediately start working on the first Sprint.

In contrast to the predictive systems and some of the adaptive systems such as DSDM®, Scrum doesn't have anything about opening and closing projects, which is considered a fundamental disadvantage by some people. Although the first Scrum resources used to have such elements, they never found their way into the Scrum Guide.

Product Backlog items
One of the main concerns in early Agile systems such as eXtreme Programming was the type of items you define for the project, because the nature of those items has a direct impact on the direction of the project. For example, it's common to limit the items to non-technical, independent user stories. (We'll discuss these attributes and the meaning of "user story" in the eXtreme Programming chapter.) Scrum, however, wants to add as few constraints as possible, and so accepts almost any type of item.

In an ideal setup where a low-tech physical board is used for the Product Backlog, each item will be on a card (index card or sticky note).

Attributes of items
Each item on the Product Backlog has these attributes:
- **Description:** This is a short description of the item. Don't try to cover all the details for the item, as these may emerge during the work. It's common to say that these items are just excuses for having conversations, rather than full specification documents.
- **Size:** We need to know the size of each item for multiple purposes. (We'll talk about that soon.)
- **Order:** The order of each item is implied by its position in the Product Backlog.

Depending on the type of project, you may want to add other attributes as well (e.g., priorities such as low, medium, and high). However, some potential attributes are not compatible with Scrum; for example, you shouldn't have an "owner" attribute for items, because their ownership is shared.

Ordering the items
The items in the Product Backlog are ordered in a way that maximizes the value of the product based on the Product Goal.

The statement above is too abstract. The actual way it can be done depends on many factors, and so it's up to the Product Owner to work out how to do it for each project.

– Non-linear nature of value
Early versions of Scrum had the idea that we can consider a certain amount of business value for each item, and it was one of the standard attributes for the items (along with description, size, and order). So, the idea was that you estimate the value of items, write them on the card, and use that to order the items. This is not completely realistic, though, because the value of each item also depends on other items you have in the product. For example, a feature for exporting content in a format compatible with Excel may be very valuable because users may want to analyze their data using Excel. However, if you add another feature for analyzing the data in your own application, users won't need to do it in Excel, and therefore, the value of the export feature drops.

Because of the non-linear nature of value explained above, value is not considered as an attribute of the items anymore, and instead of thinking of a value for each item that is the basis of ordering them, now we prefer to think of the non-linear contribution of each item to the value of the product in a more holistic approach. To be honest, a significant portion of ordering is based on the intuition of the Product Owner and their mental image of various combinations rather than on calculations.

– The definition of value
Besides the non-linear nature of value, there's another issue, which is about its definition:
- In day-to-day language, value usually refers to the benefits that result from something.
- In professional management resources (e.g., the MoV® standard for value management), value is usually defined as the benefits-to-cost ratio.

When someone talks about "value for money", they are obviously using the first definition of value, which translates to "benefits-to-cost ratio", whereas using the second definition, they can just say "value" to mean "benefits-to-cost ratio".

This is a problem for us because Agile resources in general, and Scrum in particular, use a mixture of these two definitions. When we talk about maximizing value, it must have the second definition, because it's only the benefit-to-cost ratio that should be maximized, not the benefits with any possible cost. On the other hand, the same resources state that when ordering the Product Backlog, the size of items (i.e., their cost) should be considered alongside their value, which means that they take the first definition.

– Risks, dependencies, etc.
A proper definition of "value" contains the size (cost), risks, dependencies, and other elements, and therefore, value alone would be enough for ordering the items. However, since the Scrum resources use a mixture of the two definitions for value, they usually suggest ordering the backlog based on value, size, risks, dependencies, and so on.

In general (e.g., in conversations with other people) it may be easier to just consider value, size, dependencies, risk, and other elements as the basis for ordering the items, rather than just value.

– Value-related jargon
There are some terms related to value and money that you may see in this context. Without going into details and practical applications, this is a list with a simple description for each:
- **Return on Investment (ROI):** The ROI for a specific period shows how much of your initial investment would be covered by the benefits; e.g., an ROI of 50% in 1 year means that you will recover half of your investment cost in 1 year by using the product. Higher figures for ROI are desirable. This criterion is the main one, and the commonest one in Agile projects.
- **Net Present Value (NPV):** NPV shows the total amount of investment minus the earned benefits in a specific period, with all numbers discounted to take inflation into account; e.g., an NPV of 1 million euro in 10 years means that you will earn something equal to today's 10 million euro on top of all the money you've spent on the project in 10 years. Higher figures for NPV are desirable.
- **Payback Period:** The payback period is the amount of time it takes to earn as much money with the product as you have spent on the project to create it; e.g., a payback period of 3 years means that you will break even with your investment in 3 years. Smaller payback periods are desirable.
- **Internal Rate of Return (IRR):** IRR is the discount rate at which the NPV becomes zero; e.g., if the IRR of the project is 20%, and there is a banking system with an interest rate of more than 20%, you'd be better off putting your money in that bank instead of investing it in the project.
- **Total Cost of Ownership (TCO):** The TCO is a combination of both the deployment and operation costs of the product. The point here is that if you reduce the deployment cost, you might end up with a higher operation cost, and therefore, you need to consider them together before assigning a budget to the deployment.

Size of items

Because items at the bottom of the Product Backlog will not be delivered soon, we don't need to spend time making them clear, as it's a form of detailed upfront planning. They can stay high-level and vague, and only when they move towards the top of the Product Backlog will we invest our time in making them clearer.

To make an item clearer, we need to break it down into smaller items and add more information to them. Because we only break down items that are at the top of the backlog, it's natural to have smaller items at the top of the backlog compared to the bottom. Obviously, this is a consequence of the way we refine the backlog, and it doesn't mean that we sort the backlog based on the size of items.

On the other hand, since items in the Sprint Backlog come from the top of the Product backlog, it's natural, on average, to have smaller items in the Sprint Backlog compared to the Product Backlog.

Assuming that items are user stories (which is not mandatory in Scrum – we'll talk about them in the eXtreme Programming Chapter), the larger ones are sometimes called **epic user stories**, or just **epics** for short. Those that are extremely large may be called **themes**, although, the term "theme" sometimes refers to super-large items, and sometimes to groups of related items that create a capability in the application.

Estimating items

One of the Product Backlog item attributes is size. We need to estimate the size of items for multiple purposes, including the following:

- It helps the Product Owner understand the value of the item and use that when ordering the items. For example, a feature for integrating your application with a popular platform may be very valuable if it can be done in a week, but not so desirable if it's supposed to take 6 months.
- It helps the Developers predict how many items they can pick for the Sprint Backlog during the Sprint Planning meeting.

Estimates should be done by the Developers because they are the people who will be doing the work in the future, and they know best how much effort it will take. No one else is allowed to override their estimated sizes.

Product Backlog refinement

Any form of adding detail to the Product Backlog items is called "Product Backlog refinement", or as it used to be called, "Product Backlog grooming".

The Product Owner is constantly in touch with the customer and end-user representatives, and at any time, they may discover a new requirement and create a new item for it. When they do, they go to the Developers, explain the new item, and ask them to estimate its size. This is a typical Product Backlog refinement scenario.

Another refinement scenario is that the Product Owner changes the order of the items, and some of the large items move to the top of the Product Backlog. Then, because they are now at the top, the Product Owner starts breaking them down into smaller items, either on their own or with the help of the Developers. When they are done with breaking down the items, the Developers need to estimate the size of those items.

Remember that Product Backlog refinement is not one of the Scrum events, and it's not timeboxed. It can happen at any time.

Older versions of the Scrum Guide used to suggest 10% as a typical ceiling for the amount of time the Developers spend on Product Backlog refinement. However, the 2020 version of the Scrum Guide has removed it to ensure it's not taken as a prescriptive statement. Regardless, 10% seems like a reasonable ceiling.

Ownership

It's commonly said that the Product Owner owns the Product Backlog. This means that the Product Owner is the only person who can make changes to the Product Backlog (unless they delegate some or all of this responsibility to someone else) and everyone should respect that. However, this doesn't mean that everything related to the Product Backlog is done by the Product Owner; for example, you already know that the Developers are responsible for estimating – they give the estimates to the Product Owner, and the Product Owner adds them to the items in the Product Backlog. In addition to that, many people, including the customer, influence the Product Owner in their composing the items and ordering them.

2.3.3.2 Sprint Backlog

Another Scrum artifact is the Sprint Backlog, which is our plan for the Sprint, which contains the following:
- The Sprint Goal (the answer to the **why** question)
- The Product Backlog items we've selected for the Sprint (the answer to the **what** question)
- The tasks we've created by decomposing the items (the answer to the **how** question)

The Sprint Backlog is creating during the Sprint Planning meeting, and the Developers add more details to it during the Sprint.

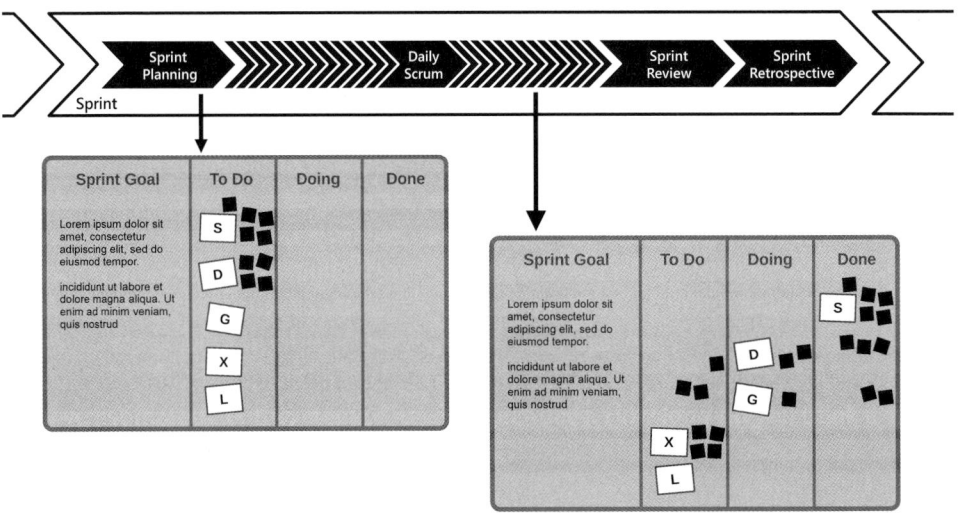

The Sprint Backlog may be managed by a software application and stored in a digital file, but we prefer to use low-tech physical boards for our Sprint Backlogs.

Ownership
The Developers own the Sprint Backlog, which means that no one other than the Developers is allowed to make changes to it. However, it doesn't mean that no one else is involved in the content of the backlog. For example, the Sprint Goal is created by the whole Scrum Team, and while the Developers decide about the number of items for the Sprint Backlog, it's primarily the Product Owner who decides which items have the highest priority and so need to be done in the Sprint.

The Sprint Goal
To make sure that our activities are fruitful, there's a Product Goal that we always use as a guide. However, the Product Goal is high-level and only satisfied in the long term. To make it more practical, there's also a Sprint Goal for each Sprint: a simpler, short-term goal that we try to attain by the end of the Sprint.

The Sprint Goal is part of the Sprint Backlog, and it usually stays fixed during the Sprint. If something happens that makes the Sprint Goal obsolete, the Product Owner has the authority to cancel the Sprint, in which case, the items will be returned to the Product Backlog and a new Sprint started. This is the only reason for cancelling Sprints.

Unfinished items
What happens if you're not done with all the items in the Sprint Backlog at the end of the Sprint? Should you panic?

You don't need to, as the items that you pick for the Sprint are just a guess. No one should blame the Developers if they couldn't deliver everything. This is because if they were blamed, they would pick fewer items, and that might result in lower productivity. Remember that the goal of the project is not to complete all the items in the Sprint Backlog, and it's not even to complete as many items as possible – the goal is to maximize the value of the product and achieve the goals.

So, what do we do with the unfinished items?

Some people move them to the next Sprint. This is not a good idea because this could happen: You may have a nice feature that seemed to be small and simple. Based on this estimate, the Product Owner sees a lot of value in having it and puts it on the top of the Product Backlog. You start working on the item during the Sprint and realize that it's much more complicated than you initially expected. When you return it to the Product Backlog at the end of the Sprint and revise its estimated size, the Product Owner may see that with the new size, the item is not attractive enough and so moves it to the middle of the Product Backlog. As a result, you won't be working on it in the next Sprint.

When an item is not finished at the end of a Sprint, we just return it to the Product Backlog, and if needed, we will revise its estimated size. Following that, the Product Owner may revise its order. In most cases, you will continue working on it in the next Sprint, but that's not always the case.

Not enough items
What would you do if you were done with all the items and you still had time left before the end of the Sprint?

It's not complicated: You could talk to the Product Owner and add one or a few more items to the Sprint Backlog. However, as you're self-managing, you may decide to spend your time investigating a new technology for the project, or improving some of the existing parts, etc.

Frozen vs. dynamic
There are three elements in the Sprint Backlog, and they have different natures. The Sprint Goal is fixed, and, normally, we don't change it in the middle of the Sprint. On the other end of the spectrum is the set of tasks that are completely dynamic; we create the first few tasks in the Sprint Planning meeting, and the rest during the Sprint.

The third element, which is the set of Product Backlog items selected for the Sprint, is a source of disagreement. Traditionally, the items are kept fixed to create a stable, distraction-free environment for the Developers. However, this traditional approach seems too rigid for some people, especially compared to iteration-free Kanban implementations. This is why many Scrum practitioners no longer believe in freezing the items for the duration of the Sprint, and it's also the approach promoted by the Scrum Guide.

2.3.3.3 Increment
Each Increment is the latest version of the application, with at least one new feature or functionality, or at least one change compared to the previous version. All Increments must be absolutely done and usable, because:
- this is the only way we can be sure that the customer and end-user representatives have a correct understanding of it and can give us reliable feedback, and
- by doing so, we will create a more predictable environment, where we can really close something and move on to the next item, without being worried that there are hidden problems in the previous stages.

This is so important that it's commonly said that the Increments must be **releasable**. We don't have to release them, but we keep them releasable to be sure they're done.

Definition of Done
It's necessary to have "done" increments that are releasable. As a result, we need to make it clear what it means for something to be done, and since it depends on the project, there can't be a general definition, and hence, the concept of the Definition of Done.

The Definition of Done is what the whole Scrum Team creates to describe what it means for increments to be done. It covers all the development processes and quality aspects (e.g., non-functional features such as performance and maintainability, tests, and coding standards).

Some organizations have quality concerns that need to be satisfied in all projects. For example, they may have a coding standard and require all projects to follow it. In that case, those organizational concerns will be added to the Definition of Done as the minimums before the team add their own conditions.

The team creates the Definition of Done at the beginning of the project and uses it throughout the project. Sometimes they learn more about the project and they can come up with improvements in the Definition of Done (e.g., during the Sprint Retrospective meeting). We prefer not to change the Definition of Done in the middle of the Sprint.

Note that the Definition of Done is about the Increment, and not about the items, because completeness of the product is an integrated concept. However, when it describes how adding a new item to the last Increment can create a new Increment that is done, it practically tells us when an individual item would be done as well.

Number of Increments
It's implied in most Agile systems that there's one Increment at the end of each iteration, and it was more or less the same in Scrum. However, they gradually distanced themselves from this system and first considered the possibility of having multiple Increments, until finally, in 2020, they made certain changes that imply there must be multiple Increments for each Sprint.

The way it's defined now is that as soon as an item is finished in a way that can be integrated with the last Increment without causing any problems for its compliance with the Definition of Done, a new Increment is formed. As a result, if you have 20 items in the Sprint Backlog and you finish all of them by the end of the Sprint, you will probably generate 20 Increments of the product (unless you finish some of them together at the same time).

The last Increment of each Sprint, which contains everything done before it, is what you review in the Sprint Review meeting. Although the Scrum Guide states that you review "the sum of all Increments", but it's no different to the last Increment from a practical point of view.

Releases
Each Increment should be releasable, but we don't have to release all of them. It's up to the Product Owner to decide when it makes sense to release the product to production. This is the responsibility of the Product Owner because releasing is a business decision that has to be aligned with the rest of the business (operations), and possibly with other projects in the organization.

In contrast to some of the other Agile systems, Scrum doesn't have a release management system. Scrum practitioners usually add their own release planning and controlling elements. Regardless of how it is done, it's the responsibility of the Product Owner, although others may help.

Any Increment can be released if it's good for the business, and it's not even limited to the last Increment of each Sprint – you can have multiple releases per Sprint if required.

2.4 Scaled Scrum

Scrum has a flat organization with no central coordination. As a result, it can't be used for too many people. When more people are needed for a project, there can be multiple teams, which is called Scaled Scrum.

There's no single, universal way of scaling Scrum, and there are multiple frameworks for this purpose, including the following:
- **Nexus™:** This is a framework from Scrum.org, with a clear and simple structure.
- **Scrum@Scale™:** This is a framework from Scrum Inc.
- **LeSS™:** This is a lightweight and straightforward scaling method with a tendency to cover the program management layer.
- **SAFe™:** This is a complicated method favored by many large organizations (e.g., banks). It's not compatible with all Agile concepts, but it satisfies the common expectations of managers in large organizations.

SAFe, and to some degree LeSS, see themselves as general scaling frameworks rather than scaling frameworks for Scrum. However, in practice, what they assume about the teams suggests that they are designed for Scrum.

Agile practitioners who need to have multiple teams also have the option of using DSDM instead of scaled Scrum, as it supports multiple teams by default.

Some Agile pioneers believe that Agile doesn't suit large projects and that scaling systems are not truly Agile, but merely a way for consultants to sell services to larger organizations. While there may be some truth to this claim, we shouldn't forget about DSDM, which is a first-generation Agile methodology that supported multiple teams and large projects by default from the beginning.

Although most of what we can say about scaling Scrum depends on the framework chosen, there are still a few general considerations, and that that's what we're going to talk about in the rest of this chapter.

2.4.1 Roles

One of the main issues in scaling Scrum is the roles – adapting the existing roles for the scaled environment, and the possibility of having extra roles. Let's take a look at the possibilities. . .

2.4.1.1 Developers

Each team has a number of Developers, but they don't have to be working full-time for a single team, and if needed, a single person can be a member of multiple teams. This is important when there's a special expertise that is needed in multiple teams but doesn't require too much time from that person.

In a default setup with one team, we prefer to have a fixed, stable team. When it comes to scaled Scrum, though, there may be more possibilities. First, some resources believe that forming the teams has to be done by the Developers themselves (probably facilitated by the Scrum Masters), which doesn't seem easy. Some resources encourage fixed teams in scaled Scrum, while some prefer to keep it flexible and let the Developers change their teams before starting each Sprint.

When forming teams, it's important to create them in such a way that each team is cross-functional and capable of completing Product Backlog items independently, or at least, without technical dependency on other teams. In general, we can think of these two types of teams:
- **Component teams:** Each team works on a certain component of the product (database, user interface, etc.).
- **Feature teams:** Each team works on the A to Z of features, independent of others.

Our preferred option is feature teams.

Sometimes, you start with one or a few teams, and then expand them into multiple teams, especially when the team members don't have a lot of experience in Scrum. In this way, they will gain some experience working in a team that knows what to do before splitting and forming a new team with one of the following two options:

- **Split-and-Seed:** The original team(s) are split into multiple teams, and new members are added to make the new teams cross-functional and powerful again.
- **Grow-and-Split:** In this case, new members are added to the existing teams until they reach their full capacity (or a little more), and then each team is split into two.

The Split-and-Seed and Grow-and-Split models are also useful for spreading and adopting the framework within the organization (for multiple projects). We can start by trying Scrum in a pilot project, and when the team becomes skilled in the Agile way of working, we can split them to create more teams and cover more projects.

2.4.1.2 Scrum Master

Each team needs to have a Scrum Master, and no more than one Scrum Master, because that's all that's needed. However, the Scrum Master role doesn't have to be full-time, and a single person can be the Scrum Master of multiple teams, which is common in practice.

A few resources suggest a new role called **Chief Scrum Master**, who coordinates all the local Scrum Masters. However, this is not common, because the Scrum Master activities don't need consistency and centralized coordination; e.g., you don't need to be worried that the way facilitation is done in one team is compatible with the way it's done in another team. For some aspects of Scrum Master activities that require consistency, we should be able to rely on their self-organized effort to achieve that, without having a separate role dedicated to coordinating them.

2.4.1.3 Product Owner

The number of Product Owners in scaled Scrum is one of the main areas of disagreement among the different frameworks:
- Some believe that there must be one and only one Product Owner, no matter how many teams there are, because the Product Owner is responsible for creating consistent items in the Product Backlog and setting priorities. This is a legitimate concern, as it's difficult to have multiple people responsible for such a thing.
- On the other hand, some frameworks believe in having one Product Owner role for each team (a single person can be the Product Owner for multiple teams) and a **Chief Product Owner** to assure consistency. The main concern in this approach is that the Product Owner is also responsible for explaining the items to the Developers and checking with them to make sure there are no surprises, and when there are many Developers, it won't be possible for a single Product Owner to do this.

2.4.1.4 Additional roles

You probably remember that additional roles are not allowed in Scrum. This rule has to be broken in scaled Scrum, though, because of our need for centralized coordination. However, some frameworks claim that they don't add additional roles, and that their seemingly additional roles are just the same Scrum Teams with different responsibilities.

As an example, Nexus has a "Nexus Integration Team" responsible for coordinating and ensuring the integration of the efforts and the Increments. This team consists of the Product Owner (there's only one Product Owner in Nexus, not one per team), a Scrum Master, and a number of other "team members" who are representatives of local, normal teams. In this example, those "team members" are playing two roles: the normal Developer role, and the representative role in the coordination layer.

2.4.2 Events
When there are multiple teams in the project, the original events need to change to adapt to it, and there may be a need for extra events.

2.4.2.1 Sprint
One straightforward method is to synchronize the Sprints, so that all teams start and end their Sprints at the same time. While this makes a lot of sense, many resources do not insist on it and allow the teams to have different Sprints. It's usually considered, though, because some teams may want to have a different timeboxed duration for their Sprints; e.g., most teams may have 4-week Sprints while a few of them have 2-week Sprints. This is still some level of synchronization, though, even if it's not called that.

If teams have completely different and incompatible Sprint lengths and start times, then managing the other events such as Sprint Reviews becomes very complicated. As a result, even for the frameworks that don't force synchronization, it's expected to have a reasonable arrangement of Sprints.

2.4.2.2 Sprint Planning
There are three topics for Sprint Planning, where team members answer the **why**, **what**, and **how** questions:
- **Why?** This results in a Sprint Goal. If we decide to have a shared Sprint Goal for all teams, then everyone is supposed to contribute and create the goal together, although the Product Owner(s) may have the biggest role here. On the other hand, the framework you use may allow different Sprint Goals, in which case it has to be

done at the team level, and it's best to have a system that ensures it's done properly. For example, if your system has multiple, local Product Owners, they are already aligned with the Chief Product Owner and work with the rest of the local team to create a local Sprint Goal. However, if you have a system with only one Product Owner and yet you want to have separate local Sprint Goals, you may run into some difficulties.

- **What?** As usual, this has to be done by the Product Owner(s) and the Developers. There are two general approaches:
  - All Developers attend the Sprint Planning meeting and work together, and each team picks items for their own team. This approach has the advantage of hearing the opinions of all team members.
  - Each team sends a representative to the Sprint Planning meeting to select items for their team. This approach has the advantage of limiting the number of participants and making the meeting more manageable.
- **How?** This part is about the items in the local Sprint Backlogs, and therefore, it has to be done locally.

Based on the explanations above, it seems necessary for any scaled system to have two parts for their Sprint Planning: a shared part for the **what** and possibly **why** topics, and a local part for the **how** (and maybe **why**) topics.

2.4.2.3 Daily Scrum

Each team has its own Daily Scrums with the default goal of synchronizing team members. Then, in one form or another, a global synchronization is needed as well, where a representative from each team (one of the Developers) attends. This helps synchronize teams with each other. Traditionally, this meeting is called the **Scrum of Scrums**, but some scaling frameworks have other names for it, and some even use the term "Scrum of Scrums" for other purposes.

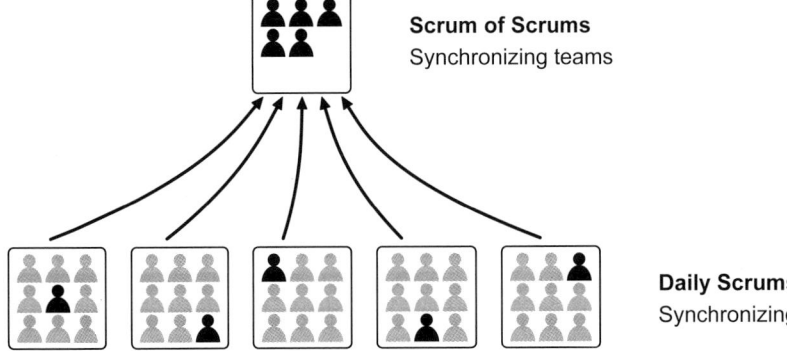

Scrum of Scrums
Synchronizing teams

Daily Scrums
Synchronizing team members

It's common for team members to answer the three classical questions during the Daily Scrum. If you want, you can have the same format for the Scrum of Scrums, in which case, you may add a fourth question: "Are you going to put something in another team's way?"

2.4.2.4 Sprint Review
This event really depends on the exact framework you're going to use. For example, it can be like this: There's a big room with all the teams and customer representatives inside it. Each team has a booth, and different customer representatives are walking around seeing the features that they have added to the integrated Increment. Alternatively, it's also possible to have a smaller meeting where each team has only one representative.

2.4.2.5 Sprint Retrospective
While the exact approach depends on the scaling framework, it seems generally necessary to have two levels of Sprint Retrospective:
- A local meeting for the team members to think about how they can improve their own team.
- A global meeting where all team members or their representatives attend and collaborate to find ways to improve the whole project.

2.4.3 Artifacts
Beside the roles already described, there also considerations regarding the artifacts, especially the Increments. We'll have a quick review of those in this section.

2.4.3.1 Product Backlog
No matter how many teams are working on the product, as long as it's about one product, there has to be one and only one Product Backlog to make sure that everything is consistent and the items are correctly prioritized.

This simple rule may not be as straightforward as expected in practice, because we may be able to break down one product into a number of smaller products, or consider a larger product that contains multiple smaller ones. To understand when we can divide something into smaller parts, call them products, and then have separate Product Backlogs for them, you can think of the practical consequences: Why do we want to have just one Product Backlog for one "product"? It's because we need to have consistency and proper prioritization. As a result, if the sub-elements of a bigger product are independent enough to be defined, prioritized, and developed separately, you can safely consider those as separate products, and so have separate projects, Product Backlogs, and teams for them.

2.4.3.2 Sprint Backlog

Each team needs to have its own Sprint Backlog, containing its own Sprint Goal, items, and tasks. In some cases you may be able to have a shared goal for all or some of the teams, which is interesting, but not mandatory and not always possible. For the items, it's necessary to have each item done by one and only one team, because otherwise there would be too many dependencies and it won't be productive. If you believe that no single team can finish an item without help from other teams, it may mean that the teams are not formed properly and they are not as cross-functional as they should be.

2.4.3.3 Increments

When we consider the special definition of Increment previously discussed, wherein each newly completed item that satisfies the Definition of Done creates a new Increment, it becomes obvious that Increments cannot belong to individual teams, but they have to be integrated and shared among all teams.

Every once in a while, a team will be nearly done with an item; they start integrating it with the rest of the code, fix broken parts and bugs, and when they are sure that everything is fine, they call it done. At that moment, a new Increment is created that contains the new item, as well as all items that all teams have created before.

In order to have a meaningful setup like the one explained above, there has to be one shared Definition of Done for all teams, to make sure that what they do is cross-compatible.

To be completely accurate, each team can create their own local Definition of Done and add their extra constraints to it. As long as their local Definition of Done is compatible with the shared definition, anything they call done will be done according to the shared definition, and there won't be a problem. This is not an uncommon case because, for example, one team may want to have extra tests in their Definition of Done because of the type of items they usually work on.

3. Crystal

Crystal is a family of Agile methodologies, including its famous lightweight version, **Crystal Clear**. It's one of the first-generation Agile methods that has contributed a lot to this domain.

We'll have a quick review of some of the key aspects of Crystal that are most common in today's Agile projects.

3.1 The Cockburn Scale

The Cockburn Scale, described by the inventor of Crystal, Alistair Cockburn, is a way of classifying projects based on their size and criticality. The idea is that the combination of these two factors determines the type of method needed for managing the project – an essential concept that seems to be forgotten in the Agile community.

The scale visualizes the concept like this:

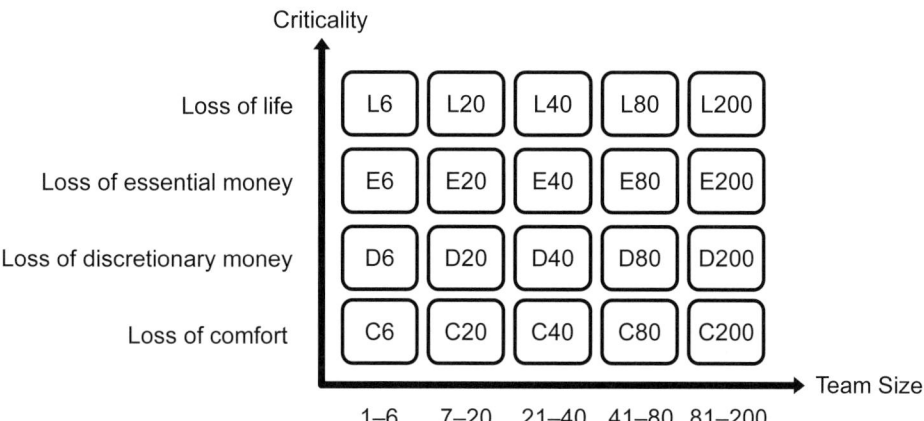

Each method can serve one or a few of these 20 classes of projects (or 16 classes in some versions), but not all of them. For example, Scrum is suitable for C6, D6, and probably E6. Cockburn himself envisioned multiple Crystal methods for subsets of these project classes, starting from Crystal Clear, which has a domain similar to Scrum, to Crystal Yellow, Orange, Red, Maroon, Diamond, and Sapphire. The only method in this family that was fully developed is Crystal Clear.

3.2 Frequent Release

Agile systems rely on adapting to the feedback instead of an upfront plan. Obviously, the success of an adaptive system depends on the quality and quantity of the feedback generated during the project.

A fact overlooked in many Agile projects is that the real feedback comes from the end-users and not the customer. You may have multiple unreleased increments of the product and review them with the customer frequently, and base everything on the feedback you receive from the customer. However, nothing guarantees that what you build like this would be successful among the real end-users. That's why it's advantageous to have releases during the project, as the real end-users will use the application and more reliable feedback will be generated.

Note that when we talk about feedback, it's not limited to asking people what they think about the increment; the most important type of feedback is observing how they use the application. Remember there's always a difference between what people say, and what they do, and the latter is more reliable.

Besides generating more reliable feedback, releasing the application to production has the advantage of generating value; i.e., the customer starts earning money.

Because of the two reasons outlined above, Crystal places great emphasis on the importance of having frequent releases. The suggestion is to have a release every few months (except for the first release, which may take longer). In the case of Web applications, the suggestion is to have releases every few weeks.

3.3 Osmotic Communication

Instead of having team members scattered throughout the organization, Crystal prefers to have our own project room and bring all the team members into one place, and have a **co-located** team.

Co-location focuses everyone on the project and makes the conversations easier. There's another advantage as well: It enables osmotic communication.

In a co-located team, there's a lot of information flowing in the background, and team members pick up relevant information automatically. For example, two developers may be discussing an issue with the authentication system, and you overhear a few sensitive keywords like "issue" and "authentication". A couple of days later, you run into an unexpected behavior in the authentication system. Instead of spending a lot of time trying to realize what's going on, you suspect that it may have something to do with the same issue they were talking about, so you go to them and start discussing it.

Osmotic communication is a direct result of co-location, but it's possible to have some level of it with virtual teams, or those scattered across multiple rooms; e.g., whenever two peers send an email to each other, they can copy in everyone else.

3.4 Walking Skeleton

A walking skeleton is a small increment of the product that can perform a simple end-to-end function.

It's desirable to create a walking skeleton as soon as possible because it's an **early victory** for the team and a demonstration of the future everyone can imagine for the product. It's also when we can show the application to non-technical people and receive their real feedback.

Some projects develop a lot without creating end-to-end functions, and it takes them a long time to have an increment that can "walk"; then when it does, it's not a skeleton anymore. It's best to arrange the development items in a way that creates those end-to-end functions as soon as possible, starting with a walking skeleton and proceeding from there.

3.5 Information Radiators

eXtreme Programming popularized the idea of **big, visible charts**, which was later adopted and expanded in Crystal with the name **information radiators** – a name that became more popular than XP's. Nowadays, some form of information radiator exists in almost every Agile project.

An information radiator is a large screen or board that shows relevant, up-to-date information about the project. People who work there or walk by can get answers to certain questions from that board without asking anyone any question.

Communicating information is key, but it's not the only function of an information radiator. It also focuses people on what they believe to be important. For example, if your goal is to increase engagement in an existing product, you may want to have an information radiator that shows the engagement ratio across time, and see how the new features you add change that.

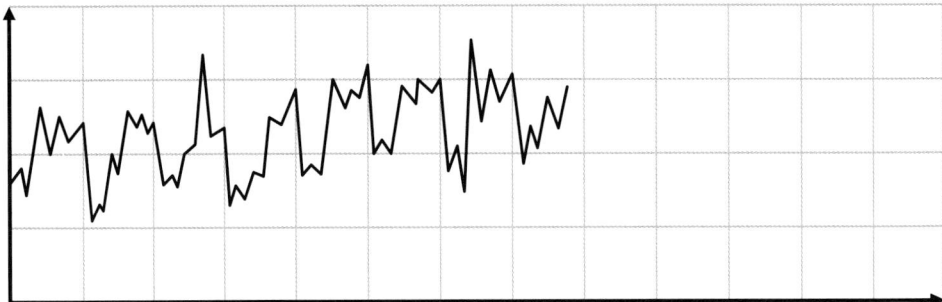

There's a rich field called **information visualization**, which covers the way you can present information to make it more useful and effective. In the example above, there's a lot of noise that makes it difficult to see the signal. For example, there's a repeating pattern that probably has something to do with the days of the week and their inherent impact on user engagement. You can show weekly values instead of daily values to remove the impact of the days of the week, and also let larger samples cancel out some of the noise.

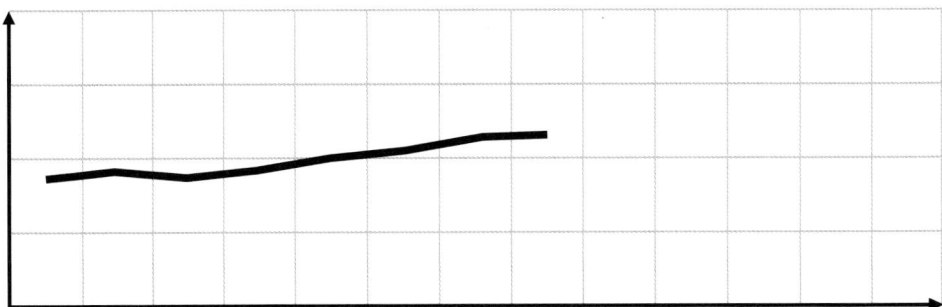

If you have a target or a few thresholds, you can add them to the chart. For example, if the typical engagement rate in your industry is 10% to 17%, you can show it as a range, and if your target is to reach 15%, you can show it as a line.

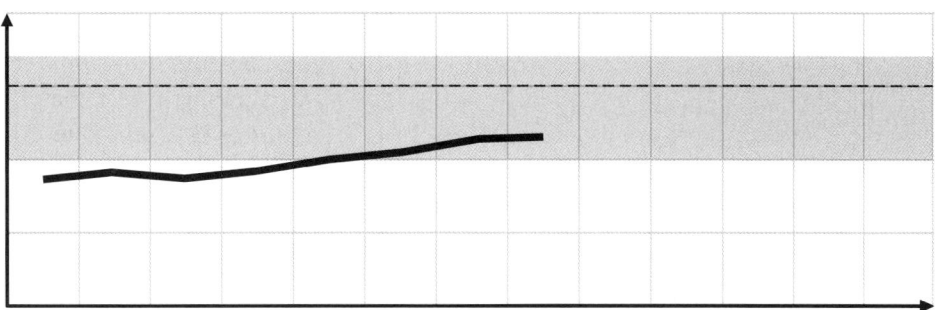

You can visualize various types of information, which we'll talk about next.

3.5.1 Escaped defects

An escaped defect is one that has escaped your test process and was discovered by the customer or end-users. Obviously, we want to minimize escaped defects as much as possible, and as a result, it may be a good idea to visualize them on an information radiator.

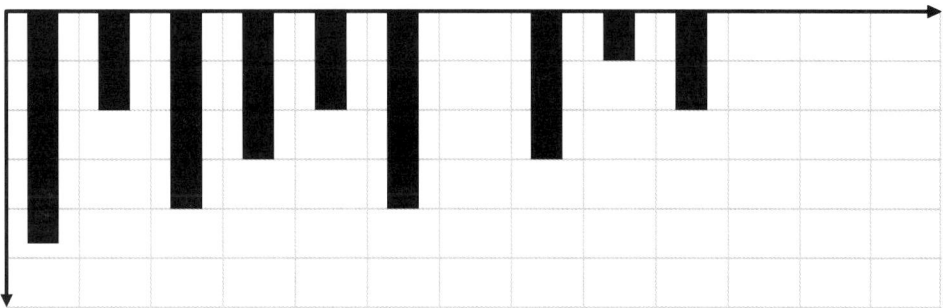

Escaped defects are undesirable, and therefore, it's best to show them as downward bars, as it shows that larger values are worse.

You can add thresholds as well, if you have any. For example, if the maximum acceptable number of defects is 5 and the desirable value is 2 or less, you can show those with two lines.

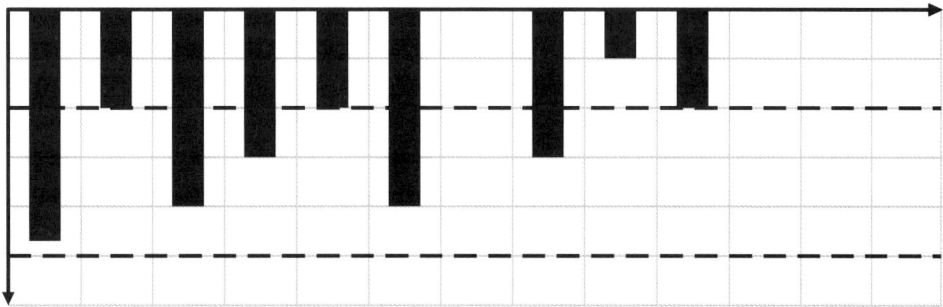

3.5.2 Progress information

What we really want to measure for progress is the value generated by our work, or how closer we've got to our goals (e.g., the Product Goal in the case of Scrum). However, those concepts are too abstract and hard to measure. As a result, we may use a proxy, and measure the amount of work done, which can be visualized in different ways, some of which we'll now go through.

3.5.2.1 Burn-up charts

One way of visualizing the amount of work done is to show the sum of the estimated size of items that are completely done across time.

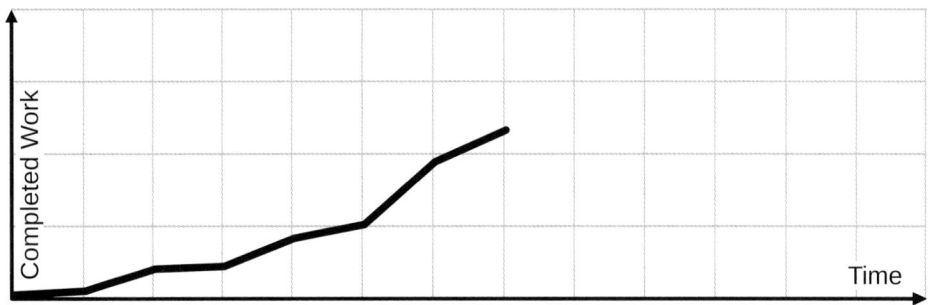

To add more signals to the chart, for example, in the case of Scrum, we can also show the target by visualizing the total size of the Product Backlog. However, because we remove the done items from the backlog, it shrinks in size, and to have a better visualization of the target, we can consider the size of the iteration plus the size of the Product Backlog (the remaining work) as the target (total work).

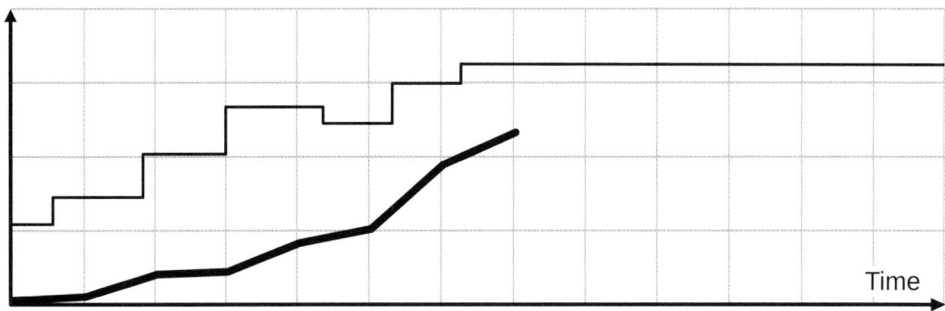

The target moves up and down as we add new items to the Product Backlog or remove items from it.

When looking at a chart like this, most people automatically think about the development rate and imagine when it will reach the target (possible completion date). So, we can make it easier for everyone by adding a trend line to the diagram:

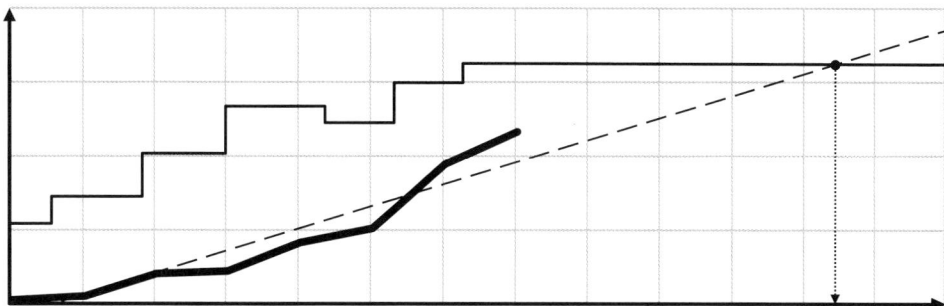

However, any Product Owner knows that a completion date like this is not reliable and only works as a simple guide, because we may change the Product Backlog at any time. To make this clearer, you can reflect it in the way the target is shown, by using a dashed line after the current date, meaning that the amount is a guess and not exact, or by replacing the line with a reasonable range.

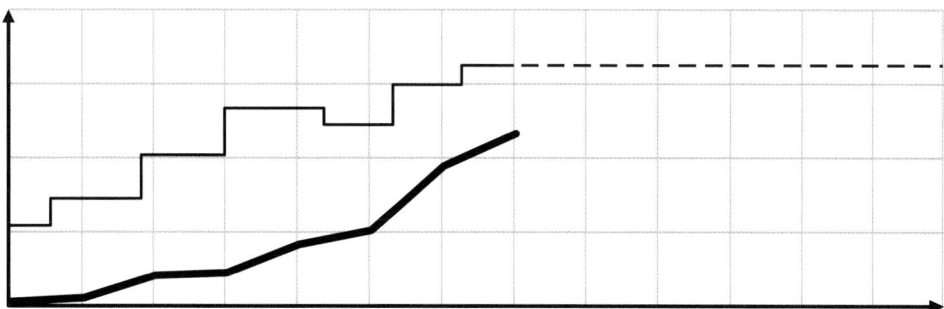

Finally, if you have specific milestones, it would be helpful to show them on the chart. For example, a release that is planned based on the approximate completion of the product can be shown by the horizontal line, and a release planned by a fixed date can be shown by a vertical line.

3.5.2.2 Burn-down charts

You can reverse the previous chart and show it like this:

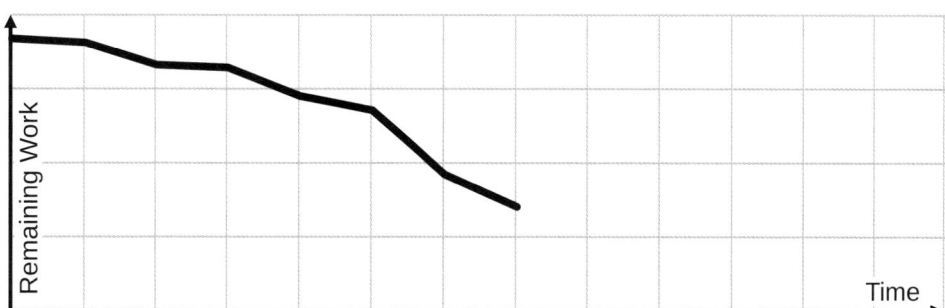

Instead of showing the amount of work done, this chart shows the amount of work remaining. Because the line goes down as you progress, it's called a burn-down chart.

Burn-down charts became popular in Scrum projects and they are still the most popular way of visualizing progress, despite their serious flaws. They are so common that the Agile community knows the normal type of chart (the previous type) as a "burn-up chart" just because it's the reverse form of the burn-down chart.

The first problem with the burn-down chart is from the information visualization perspective: Progress is desirable, and it's more intuitive for desirable things to go up rather than down.

The second problem is that burn-down charts work fine when the amount of work is fixed, but if the amount of work changes, then you will have to keep adjusting the vertical axis. This type of diagram was primarily used for tracking the progress of Sprints, and Sprints used to have a fixed set of items, and so there wasn't a problem with moving targets. One could simply add a vertical line to show the timeboxed end of the Sprint, and draw a trend line to see whether everything can be finished by the end of the Sprint.

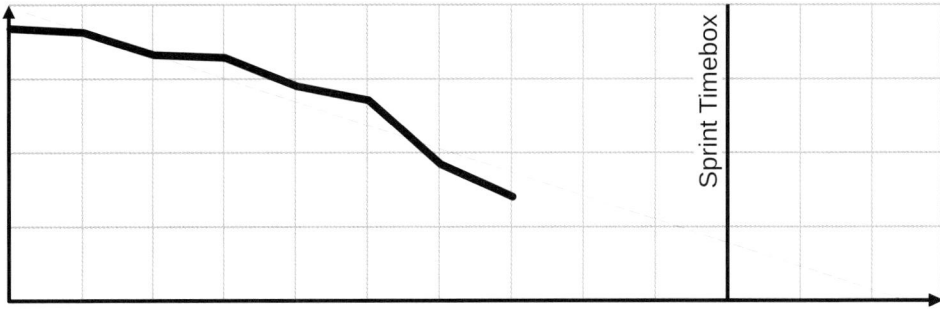

Instead of a trend line (or in addition to it), you can draw a simple line that represents a linear rate that brings you from the start to the end. It can be considered as the planned progress, and you can check to see your performance by comparing the actual value to the planned one: If the actual line is above the plan, you're behind schedule; otherwise, you're ahead of schedule.

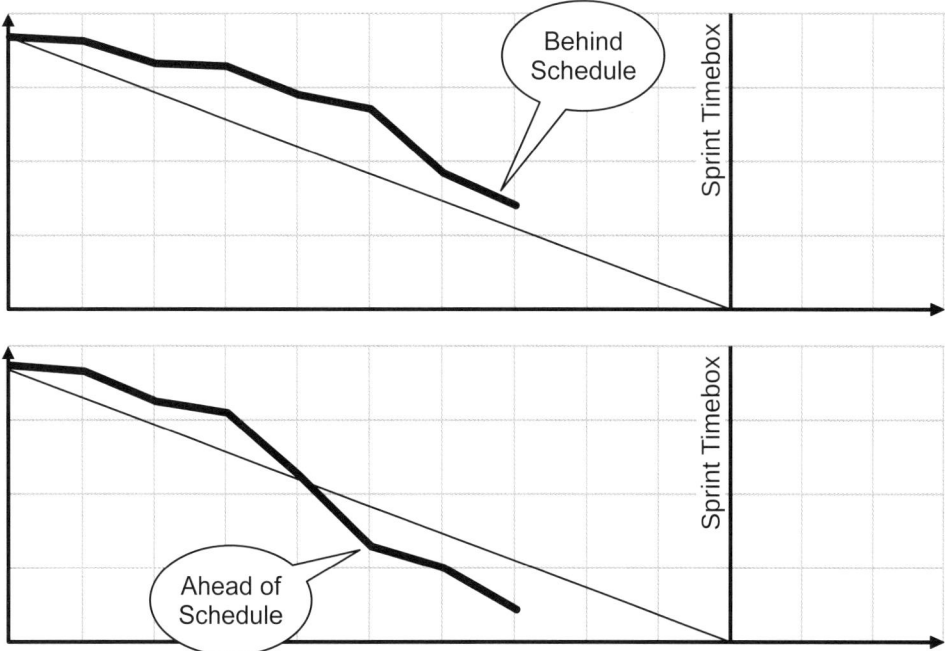

Progress charts like this can be used for tracking the progress of Sprints as well as of the project as a whole, but burn-down charts are not good enough when used for the whole project because there's no fixed target.

3.5.2.3 Burn-down bars

Burn-down charts work more or less fine for the Sprints because they have fixed targets, but cause problems when used for the project as a whole, because the Product Backlog constantly changes. Since it's difficult to keep adjusting the vertical scale, and even if we do adjust it, the rate of those changes won't be visible on the chart, one response is to make the adjustment to the bottom of the chart, by adding bars that show the amount of remaining work.

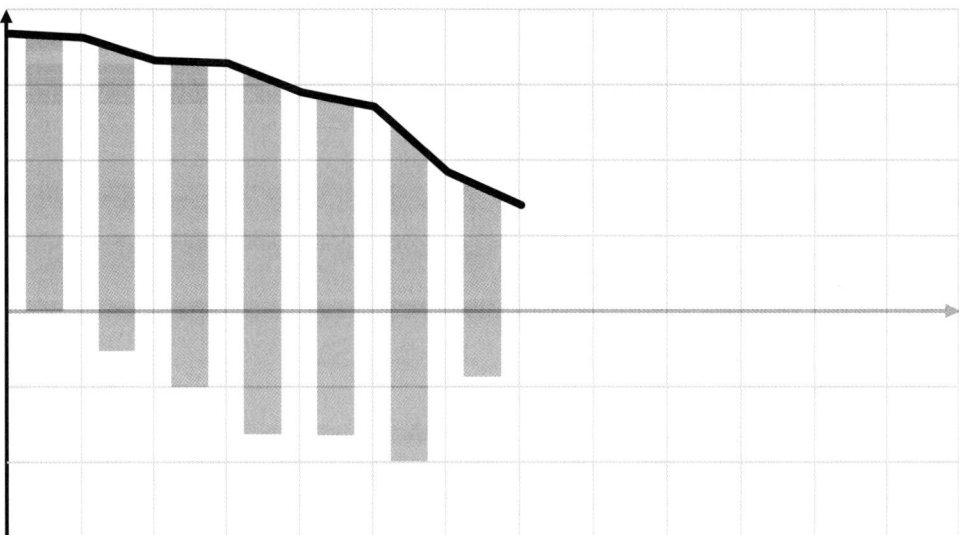

In a diagram like this, which is called a burn-down bar, if you add new items to the Product Backlog or remove items from it, the bottom of the bar goes either down or up, and when you finish something, it will impact the top of the bar and the line.

You can draw a trend line, and this time, you will have to compare it with either the last bar (the last state of the Product Backlog) or a more complicated target that considers the possible changes to the backlog.

This type of chart may help with some of the problems of burn-down charts, but it has its own problems. The simplest solution is to use a normal upward diagram (what people in the Agile community call a burn-up chart).

3.5.2.4 Cumulative flow diagrams

Let's say you're drawing a normal upward diagram to show the progress of the project one iteration at a time. You can draw it as a line diagram to emphasize the trend, as a cumulative bar chart to emphasize the contribution of iterations, or as a cumulative area chart to emphasize the flow of the process.

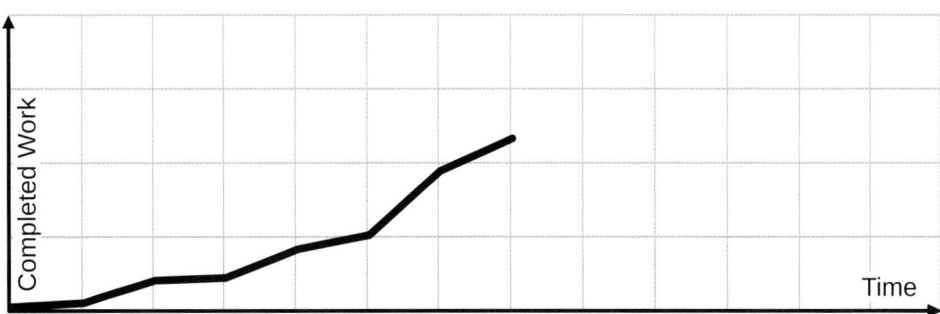

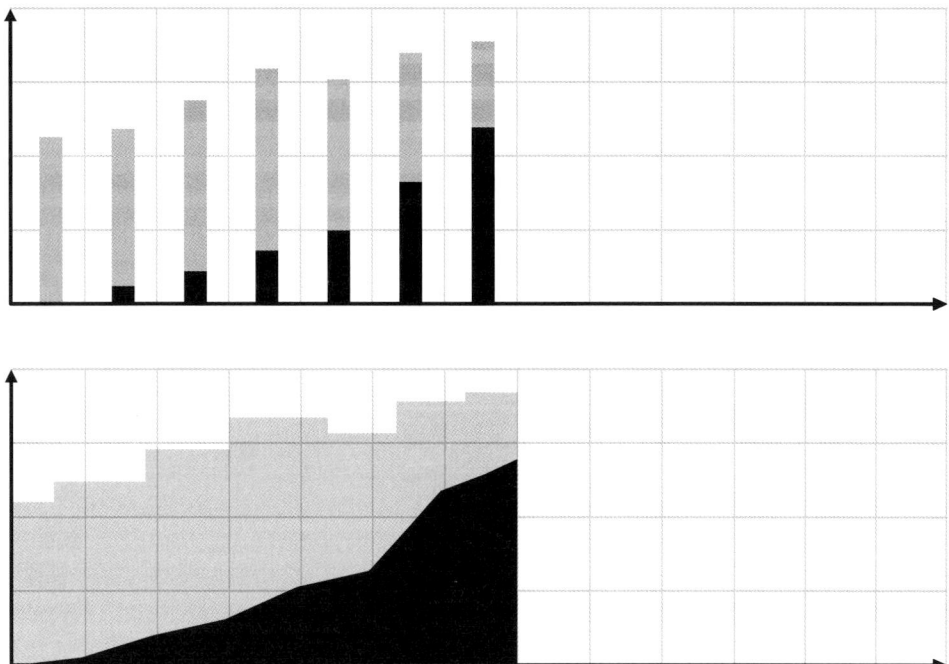

The area chart with the emphasis on the flow is called a **cumulative flow diagram**, which is a common chart in Kanban. It's mainly used when measurements are not limited to the "to do" and "done" states like the example above, but also track different steps of work, such as design, programming, and testing. Such a chart can show potential bottlenecks.

3.5.3 Niko-Niko calendar

Another type of information radiator that some people use is the Niko-Niko calendar, which visualizes the morale of team members. Each team member visualizes their mood by selecting an emoticon at the end of each day.

In a Scrum project, if you're a Scrum Master and realize that people may hesitate to report their mood, maybe you can build a system that receives it anonymously and adds it to the chart without names, in order to give you more reliable data. Then, you can try to correlate the overall mood with the events in the project and see whether you need to take any action to help the team.

4. eXtreme Programming

Scrum is Agile, but Agile is not Scrum.

In other words, Scrum is not the only Agile option. A very powerful and practical alternative is eXtreme Programming (XP), which used to be the most popular one at the beginning but is not so common anymore.

In this chapter, we're going to review some aspects of XP, which is a great source of **Agile practices** that can also be used in other Agile systems such as Scrum. However, note that this content about XP is simplified to match the level of this book, and there are a lot more interesting, practical details in it that you can find in resources that are specifically about XP.

4.1 Daily Routine

There's a typical **daily routine** in XP projects that explains a normal development day and the way in which Agile practices can be used together in an integrated way. Let's have a look.

4.1.1 Pairing
The first thing you do in the morning is pair up! Yes, developers work in pairs in XP.

This is how it works: The two developers sit beside each other, in front of one computer. One person is coding, and the other is observing and giving comments. Every once in a while (e.g., every 30 minutes) they switch places.

This is called **pair programming**, and it is one of the XP practices.

Pair programming may seem strange, and many managers think that it's a waste of resources. However, it's financially justifiable for the following reasons:
- It increases the quality of the work, which will prevent costly future reworks.
- It helps increase the expertise of the developers.
- It helps increase the **bus factor** of the team.
- It's a continuous team-building activity.

So, what's the bus factor?

Imagine that one of the developers leaves the building and, sadly enough, gets hit by a bus and passes away. If this tragedy blocks the whole project because there are aspects of it that no one else understands, the project is said to have a bus factor of 1. If, in the worst case, it takes two bus accidents to block the project, it has a bus factor of 2, and so on. Having a low bus factor is always risky.

So, we use pair programming in XP, and therefore, the first thing we do every day is pair up – preferably in a new pair, rather than the same one over and over again.

4.1.2 Assignment

After pairing up, the pair goes to the project board and selects one of the high-priority items that matches their expertise.

Remember that no one assigns work to developers – it's up to them to do so. A common misunderstanding in many Scrum projects is that their Scrum Masters or Product Owners come to the team and assign work to the developers.

Moreover, even though a pair of programmers becomes responsible for the item, everyone in the team stays accountable for the item. This is the same in Scrum and other Agile methods. This is called **collective code ownership**, which means that anyone can make changes to any part of the code, and no single developer (or subset of developers) can claim ownership for any part of it.

So, the pair have selected an item from the board. What next?

4.1.3 Design

After selecting the item, the pair go in front of a whiteboard and start working on the design of the item.

Another XP practice is **simple design**, which results in a code that has these attributes:
- It runs all the tests.
- It contains no duplicate code.
- It states the programmer's intent for all the code clearly.
- It contains the fewest possible classes and methods.

In addition to that, it's not an upfront design at the beginning of the project – it's done when you're ready to develop the item.

So, shall we start programming now?

4.1.4 Write test
Another XP practice is **test-driven development**, which is also called test-first development. In this approach, we create the tests first, which are failing tests at this point, and then write as much code as is needed to pass the tests.

Test-driven development has multiple advantages, including the following:
- It keeps everyone focused on the problem they are going to solve.
- You always have a complete set of tests for the whole system, so, every time you add a new feature or make changes to the existing ones, you can easily run the tests and make sure the integrated system works fine and nothing is broken in the old code.

Another XP practice is **continuous integration**, in which new code is continuously integrated with the old. You can see how test-driven development helps with continuous integration.

Test-driven development requires discipline. In the beginning, it may be faster to work without it, but, in the long run, it's probably faster and results in a higher-quality, more maintainable solution.

One way to formulate test-driven development is with the following rules:
- You're not allowed to write any production code unless it is to make a failing unit test pass.
- You're not allowed to write any more of a unit test than is sufficient to fail, and compilation failures are failures.
- You're not allowed to write any more production code than is sufficient to pass the one failing unit test.

As you can guess by reading the above rules, writing tests and writing the code is iterative. You don't write all the tests that are needed for the function and then start working on the code, but you write one test, plus a little code to pass it, and then the next test and a little more code, and so on.

4.1.5 Code
So, when you have a failing test in your test-driven development approach, you can start coding until you pass the test. As mentioned, you need to do it iteratively, until all tests are written and passed in order to satisfy the feature.

While you're coding, you should also remember the **coding standards** practice. Yes, XP is full of "practices".

The coding standards practice states that you should have a standard way of coding (e.g., naming conventions) that makes it uniform and easy for every developer to understand.

When you're done with coding and the new feature is working fine, you'll go on to the next step.

4.1.6 Refactor

It's time for another XP practice: **refactoring**.

Refactoring is improving the code without changing its external behavior.

At this point, you're done with the code, and it's working. However, you still refactor it. You go through the code to see how you can make it simpler and improve its structure. Do you see how this is connected with the practice of simple design?

How can you be sure you're not breaking anything while refactoring, though? It's simple: You're using test-driven development and therefore, you have a full set of automated tests that you can run after every change to make sure nothing is broken.

If you don't refactor the code, the troubling elements remain there and sooner or later they will cause you problems. If you do it immediately, you still remember every detail about the code and it will be done very easily and quickly, but if you ignore it, when you're forced to come back to it after a few months, you have to work a lot more to discover and fix the problems. It's like having a debt that you must pay: You either pay it right away or pay it later with its additional interest. (The interest rate is really high!) This debt is called **technical debt**, and refactoring is one way of reducing it.

4.1.7 Integrate

Another practice in XP is **continuous integration**. You don't wait until the end of the iteration or approaching the release time to integrate the code, but you do it immediately after refactoring (or even before it). This is helpful because each time you integrate the code, something may break, and it's always easier to fix it when you're still actively involved with that part of the code. Furthermore, it also helps keep the output more reliable, as you know exactly how much work is done, and it makes it possible to show it to the customer and end-user representatives and receive reliable feedback.

The last person who adds something to the integrated code and breaks it is responsible for fixing it, which is an implication of the **collective code ownership** practice.

If you can't fix it by the end of the day, you will roll back the changes and continue the next day.

4.1.8 Go home!

XP used to have a practice called the **40-hour work week**, which was against overtime work. Later on, it was renamed as something more appropriate, and now we have the **constant pace** practice.

The point is that you have certain working hours such as 9 to 5, and just don't extend it. If you're done by 5, good. Otherwise, you roll back the changes to the integrated code and continue the next day.

This practice helps improve the quality of life, and consequently, the quality of the product.

4.1.9 Stand-up meetings

The previous activities of the daily routine were sequential (although, writing tests and coding are done iteratively in a loop), but there are non-sequential activities as well. The first one is the stand-up meeting.

The stand-up meeting is a 10- to 15-minute daily meeting for the developers to get together and see what's going on in the project. It's done standing up to make sure they do it quickly, and it's held at the same time and place every day to make it more regular and avoid the unnecessary overhead of arranging meetings.

During the meeting, each developer tells everyone what they were doing the day before, what they are going to do on the current day, and what problems they are encountering. Note that the goal is to communicate problems, not to solve them.

Do you remember the name of the Scrum meeting similar to this?

4.1.10 Tracking

The other element in the daily routine is tracking performance. One of the developers has the role of **Tracker**, and is responsible for this measurement, which probably needs the collaboration of the other developers as well.

It's a good idea to frequently change the person assigned to the Tracker role.

4.1.11 Risk management

Another role is the **Doomsayer**. This person encourages everyone to think about the risks and problems, and then the whole team collaborates to see how they can manage those risks or problems.

4.2 Spiking

Now that we're done reviewing the daily routine, let's have a look at a few other concepts, starting with one that has a lot to do with the daily routine: spiking. Spiking is a common term in Agile that refers to any type of research or prototyping that can help with future developments.

The exact meaning of spiking is a little different in XP. As you may remember, we use test-driven development, coding standards, continuous integration, and a few other practices in XP that create a very disciplined way of working. This way of working is great for the actual development, but not for trying out ideas.

So, sometimes, you're spiking instead of doing the actual work. When you do so, you just write code without following the practices. You write a quick and dirty piece of code for the purpose of trying out an idea or technology. The rule is that you shouldn't keep this code! When you're done with the code and have learned what you wanted to, you delete the code and get back to the standard way of working.

4.3 The Nature of Items

The nature of the work items that will be built (e.g., Product Backlog items in Scrum) is crucial. Different types of items entail different ways of working, and not every one of them enables adaptation. Check out these examples:
1. Users should be able to reset their passwords.
2. Sysadmins should be able to block users' access if needed.
3. The database should be backed up automatically every night.
4. Database tables that serve data to performance-sensitive parts of the application should be denormalized.
5. The whole system should be GDPR compliant.

Can you distinguish the different types of items?

The first three items are non-technical, functional features. You can easily talk to your non-technical customer about them, and demonstrate how they work. The last two items are technical and more or less non-functional – there's no straightforward way of demonstrating them to the customer.

Non-functional features are those related to performance, security, maintainability, scalability, and similar attributes. They are about the way functional features work.

The last two items tend to create a sequential development approach similar to the predictive projects, while we want to have an adaptive approach based on functions.

That's why we normally prefer to have items similar to the first three, and let the other types of work be done while we're working on the functional features. For example, in the case of GDPR compliance, instead of having an item for it, you can add it to your Definition of Done, and whenever you create a new feature, check to make sure that it's GDPR compliant as well.

While Scrum doesn't dictate any constraints on the type of items on the Product Backlog, Agile practitioners and especially XP users have been concerned about it and they have developed a certain approach, which will be reviewed next.

4.3.1 The two rules
There's an old-fashioned, XP-style approach to composing the items in which each item should have the following two characteristics:
- Non-technical;
- Independent.

Being non-technical is important because it makes it possible for everyone involved in the project, including the non-technical business people, to understand the items and turn the whole list of items (e.g., Product Backlog in the case of Scrum) into a source of mutual understanding for the project. It also makes it possible to demonstrate the newly developed items.

You may be asking yourself how we can do technical things like setting up the database when we limit ourselves to technical items. The answer is that you will do them as soon as you need them for a non-technical item, and you usually do as much of it as is needed for having that item up and running, and no more.

Having items that are independent is important because if there's any dependency, we won't be able to order the items freely and will have to constantly check their dependencies. To make it possible, you may have to recompose the items or merge some of them in a way that eliminates dependencies.

Sometimes it's difficult to remove all the dependencies, but experience shows that at least most of them can be eliminated when the items are composed properly. Also, note that when we talk about dependencies, it's about those that can block the development of items, not dependencies in the natural way of using the software. For example, is there a dependency between the following two items?
1. A feature to let people open a new user account in the system;
2. A feature to let people reset their passwords.

In the natural use of the application, we need to be able to create user accounts before having the need or possibility to reset passwords. However, when it comes to development, there's no real dependency between these two, because we can always add the user accounts to the database manually, and check to see whether the feature for resetting passwords works OK.

As usual, Scrum doesn't force these rules, but rather leaves it to the practitioners to decide how they want to compose their Product Backlog items.

4.3.2 INVEST
As an alternative to the previous two rules, there's a recommendation formulated as **INVEST**, which suggests six characteristics for each item:
- **Independent:** We want the items to be independent of each other to be able to develop them based on their importance and value without being worried about their dependencies.
- **Negotiable:** Product Backlog items are also communication tools and they should be negotiable.
- **Valuable:** Each item contributes to the value of the product, which is normally the basis for the order of development.
- **Estimate-able:** We need a simple estimation of size for each item; if an item doesn't seem estimate-able, there may be something wrong with the framing of the item.
- **Small:** Only the items at the top of the list have to be small; it is OK for the rest of them to be big, or even unclear.
- **Testable:** If it doesn't seem possible to demonstrate and test the item, there's something wrong with the framing of the item.

Scrum doesn't force any of these rules.

4.3.3 User stories
Based on the concerns discussed before, XP practitioners used to limit their items to those that communicate a **story** instead of those that resemble a technical specification. For example:

```
Some users who open their accounts using their corporate email
address may leave that company, and therefore, they need to
change the email address of their user account to their personal
address. We need to make it possible, while making sure that
proper authorization is done before making any changes.
```

Some stories are long, like the one above, and some can be really short, such as the following:

```
Users should be able to reset their passwords.
```

The only thing in common among all of them is that they have a story, which means that they are not technical and describe a function, and that they don't contain all the details, but are triggers for conversations and explorations.

Gradually, the free-style form of stories evolved into a pattern that is now called the **user story**:

> As a {role}, I want to {do something}, [in order to {purpose}].

The third element is optional because the purpose of some stories is too obvious; for example:

> As a user, I want to reset my password.

However, when it's not obvious, it's helpful to add the purpose to make sure there will be no misunderstanding:

> As a shop manager, I want to receive a report on the number of abandoned carts, to analyze the reasons and find ways to increase sales.

Or...

> As the sysadmin, I want to bock a user to prevent suspicious or harmful activities.

Some statements may match the pattern of user stories, while not having a real story behind them, which makes them undesirable. For example:

> As the admin, I want to have a SQL database for the application. (Incorrect!)

The last example is not appropriate because it doesn't have a function and forces a technical decision into the format of a user story.

Nowadays, most Agile practitioners assume that every item (e.g., Product Backlog item in the case of Scrum) has to be a user story, and they even use the term "user story" to refer to the work items (even when their items are not really user stories). In general, limiting ourselves to either the original free-style type of stories or the modern user story patterns is a good idea.

4.4 Estimating

There are two main reasons for estimating the size of items:
1. It helps the team forecast how many of the high-priority items they can select for their iteration.
2. It helps forecast the completion date of releases and the whole project.

Estimating is not easy, though. There are many pitfalls in estimating, and the Agile community in general and XP practitioners in particular have gradually developed methods that can reduce those risks. That's what we're going to review next.

4.4.1 Ideal-time

Estimating duration is risky because we can never be sure when something might be finished, especially when we have an adaptive system where the details of items are not completely clear before starting to develop them. As a result, XP practitioners gradually started using more abstract ways of measurement that don't create unrealistic expectations for the customer and other stakeholders.

The first solution was to estimate items in **ideal-time** instead of actual time:

```
This item takes 3 ideal-days.
```

It means that if we're in a good mood, we're not distracted at all, we don't have any meetings or conversations scheduled with anyone, there's no small urgent thing to do, and everything is in its ideal state, it will take us 3 days to finish the work. However, we never reach that ideal state, and therefore, the actual elapsed duration is always longer than the ideal duration.

4.4.1.1 Relationship with time

Let's say the team has estimated the following items in ideal-days and then gradually finished them, and we know the elapsed durations:

```
Item #1    2 ideal-days    3 days
Item #2    1 ideal-day     1 day
Item #3    4 ideal-days    5 days
Item #4    3 ideal-days    5 days
Item #5    2 ideal-days    3 days
```

They've estimated another item to need 6 ideal-days. How long do you think it would take them to finish it?

It's realistic to assume that they will have the same efficiency as before. In the past, they have completed 12 ideal-days worth of work in 17 days, and therefore the efficiency of their actual days is about 70% (12÷17). This also shows their development speed, and we can say that their **velocity** is 0.7 ideal-days per day; or if their iterations are 22 working days, we can say that their velocity is about 15 ideal-days per iteration (0.7×22).

How long would it take them to develop a 6-ideal-day item? It would probably be a little more than 8 days (6÷0.7).

4.4.1.2 Self-correction

If there was supposed to be a fixed conversion between the ideal-days and days (the way there is, for example, between the Celsius and Fahrenheit scales), there would have been different scales for the same thing, and using ideal-days instead of days wouldn't have made much difference. However, this is not the case. Let's say we've continued working, and these are the latest results:

```
Item #1     2 ideal-days    3 days
Item #2     1 ideal-day     1 day
Item #3     4 ideal-days    5 days
Item #4     3 ideal-days    5 days
Item #5     2 ideal-days    3 days
Item #6     1 ideal-days    2 days
Item #7     4 ideal-days    2 days
Item #8     3 ideal-days    2 days     (yes, it's possible!)
Item #9     6 ideal-days    7 days
Item #10    4 ideal-days    5 days
```

At this moment in time, our efficiency has increased to ~85%, which makes our velocity about 0.85 ideal-days per day. This could have happened because we've improved how we interact with the customer, for example.

The same 6-ideal-day item that was previously estimated to take 8 days, would take about 7 days (6÷0.85) if we do it now because we're more efficient now. What it means is that we can estimate the items once, independent of our efficiency. Based on our last velocity, the equivalent time required for each ideal-day will be adjusted automatically. We can say that ideal-time is a **self-correcting** unit.

In contrast to the Celsius and Fahrenheit scales, which measure the same thing (temperature), ideal-days and days don't depict the same phenomenon; ideal-days is about the size of items and the amount of effort required for completing them rather than the amount of time required to complete them. Hence, we can say that an ideal-day, despite its misleading name, is an **effort-based** unit and not a **time-based** unit.

4.4.2 Story points
Ideal-days was a good solution for two reasons:
1. It could prevent unrealistic expectations by avoiding a time-based unit.
2. It could simplify estimation because it was self-correcting.

However, the name "ideal-days" implies that it has something to do with time, and using the efficiency measurement could imply that the team is not as efficient as it could be. As a result, XP teams started replacing the phrase "ideal-days" with abstract names such as **gummy bears**! So, they used to say "This item is 4 gummy bears", and when asked, they would have replied that it's a relative unit and its relationship with time depends on the current **velocity** of the team.

Gradually, abstract names such as gummy bears were replaced with a more neutral, general name: **points**. Since items were usually stories, the unit came to be known as **story points**.

Story points were initially the same as the ideal-days, but the abstract name helped teams give it a more abstract definition that is not dependent on time at all (not even ideal time). The story point became a fully abstract, relative unit for measuring the size of items or the amount of effort required to develop them.

4.4.2.1 Estimating in story points
To keep story points abstract and relative, the modern way of estimating them is to define a simple, understandable story as the definition of one story point. Then, whenever we want to estimate a new story, we will compare it with the reference and give it a relative value. If the target story seems to be 10 times bigger than the reference, it would be 10 story points.

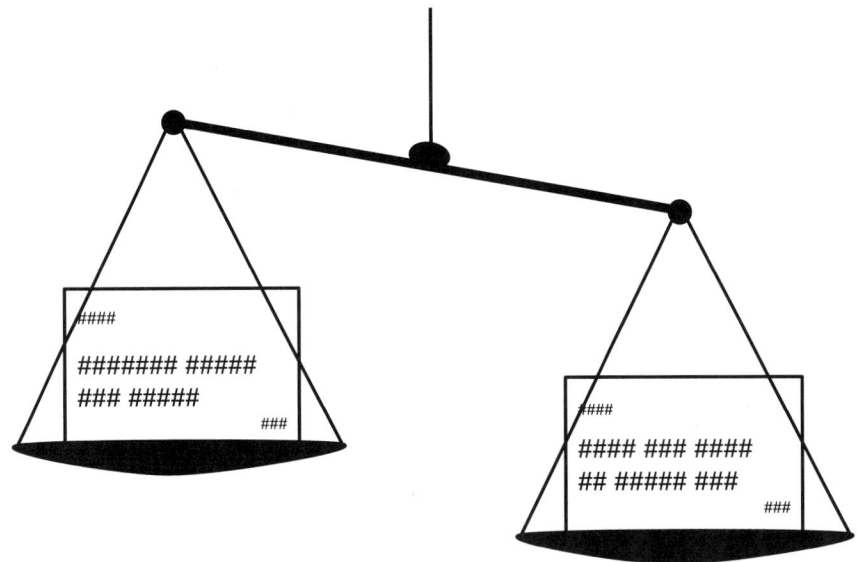

4.4.2.2 Relationship with time

At any point in time, the team has a **velocity**, using which we can convert story points to time. For example, take the following as the cumulative performance of the team:

```
Item #1          8 story points          2 days
Item #2          5 story points          1 day
Item #3         22 story points          5 days
Item #4         14 story points          4 days
Item #5          8 story points          3 days
```

Based on these outputs, we've completed 57 story points in 15 days, which means that our velocity is about 3.8 story points per day (57÷15).

If an item is estimated as 42 story points, at this point in time, our best guess is that it would take about 11 days (42÷3.8).

4.4.2.3 Self-correction

Similarly to ideal-time, our velocity always changes, and it will change the way we convert story points to time. For example, this may be our performance after a while:

```
Item #1          8 story points          2 days
Item #2          5 story points          1 day
Item #3         22 story points          5 days
Item #4         14 story points          4 days
Item #5          8 story points          3 days

Item #6          1 story points          0.5 day
Item #7          5 story points          1 day
Item #8         32 story points          5 days
Item #9         18 story points          3 days
Item #10        12 story points          1.5 days
```

At this time, we've completed 125 story points in 26 days, which makes our velocity 4.8 story points per day (125÷26).

With this new level of performance, the same 42-story-point item that would have taken about 11 days before would take about 9 days now (42÷4.8) because we've become faster.

4.4.3 T-shirt sizes

Some teams that are new to Agile are uncomfortable with the idea of using an abstract, relative, effort-based unit. If forced to use one, some of their members would think about the amount of time it takes to do the item and then convert it back to story points, which is not correct.

To avoid this problem, they can start estimating in T-shirt sizes (XXS, XS, S, M, L, XL, XXL) instead of numbers. It's still a relative, effort-based unit of size, and chances are lower that they would think of time when estimating.

The low granularity of T-shirt sizes may seem inadequate, but the fact is that this rough estimate is enough for most of the purposes, and it works fine.

4.4.4 Velocity

We've seen what velocity means and how it's used in the project. There are two main uses for it:
1. Estimating the number of items the team can take for the iteration;
2. Estimating the completion date of the project, or of releases.

4.4.4.1 Planning iterations

Velocity is the average amount of work (in ideal-time, story point, or any other unit) done in a unit of time. Anything can be used as the unit of time, such as days or iterations. The most common choice is to calculate the velocity for iterations and say, for example, "Our velocity is 650 story points per iteration right now."

If your velocity is 650 story points per iteration, when it's time to plan a new iteration, you will probably select a number of items that are roughly equivalent to 650 story points. Regardless of that, remember that it's all up to the developers to decide how many items they want to select; it can be worth 400 story points or 900 story points, despite having a velocity of 650 story points per iteration.

A phrase like "ideal-days" can be a shorthand for "ideal-team-days", "ideal-person-days", or even when you use pair programming, for "ideal-pair-days". When not specified, ideal-days usually means ideal-person-days. Besides ideal-days, we can use ideal-hours and other similar units as well.

When it comes to planning a new iteration, if iterations are 22 working days and there are 10 developers in the team, their capacity for the iteration would be 220 person-days, and if their efficiency is 85%, 220 person-days would be equivalent to about 190 ideal-person-days (220×0.85). Therefore, when it's time to start a new iteration, they will probably take a number of items that are worth approximately 190 ideal-person-days.

Planning the upcoming iteration based on the overall velocity or the velocity of the past few iterations is one option, and the other option is to simply pick a number of items roughly equivalent to what was completed in the last iteration. The latter method is called **yesterday's weather**. This name is based on a relatively old story of an expensive weather forecast application that was developed and had a forecast accuracy of 70%. Not long after the launch, people noticed that you can get the same 70% accuracy by simply forecasting that each day's weather will be the same as the day before.

Remember that in every project, and especially Agile ones, the goal is not to have the most accurate values, but to have a level of accuracy that is suitable for the purpose. This is a topic that is also reflected in the fifth principle of the Nearly Universal Principles of Projects (https://nupp.guide).

4.4.4.2 Estimating the completion date

Let's say there are 150 items remaining in the backlog, with a total size of 820 story points. If our currency velocity is 90 story points per iteration, we can forecast that the project would be finished in about 9 iterations (820÷90). However, there's an important assumption here: It will be finished in about 9 iterations if we don't add new items to the backlog and don't remove the existing items. Is this assumption valid? Usually not. However, the person responsible for the backlog (e.g., the Product Owner in Scrum) usually has an idea of the amount of change likely in the future. They would use the 9 iteration forecast as a guide and then adjust it based on other information to come up with a reasonable forecast.

4.4.4.3 Performance measurement

A common misunderstanding in Agile projects is to consider velocity as a measure of the performance of the team. This is not correct because velocity is only about speed, and our goal is not about developing as much as possible, but it's all about maximizing value and achieving the project goals. Incorrect measurements mislead the team and distract them from what they really need to pay attention to. Velocity should never be tracked as a measure of the performance of the team.

4.4.4.4 Comparing velocities

Another misunderstanding about velocity is comparing the velocity of one team with that of another. This is not correct because firstly, we don't need to compare performance – we don't want to blame any person or team for low performance, but we want to enable them and let them do their best. Secondly, the velocity of each team depends on the definition they have for story points (if they work in different projects), the number of people in the team, the type of items they're working with, and many more factors, and therefore, the velocity of one team cannot be compared with that of another.

4.4.4.5 Unfinished work vs. velocity

Let's say this is what we've done in the firs iteration:

```
Item #67         10 story points     100% done
Item #143         5 story points     100% done
Item #81         22 story points     100% done
Item #209         8 story points     100% done
Item #44         10 story points      90% done
Item #5           4 story points      50% done
Item #99         12 story points       0% done
```

What's our velocity at the end of this iteration?

The first thing we have to do is to fix the list. We don't measure the percentage of completeness – we only have done or not done.

```
Item #67         10 story points     done
Item #143         5 story points     done
Item #81         22 story points     done
Item #209         8 story points     done
Item #44         10 story points     ----
Item #5           4 story points     ----
Item #99         12 story points     ----
```

When calculating velocity, only the done items are counted. As a result, our output is 45 story points (10+5+22+8) for one iteration, which makes our velocity 45 story points per iteration. Let's say we continue the project and this is the result at the end of the second iteration:

```
Iteration #1
   Item #67         10 story points     done
   Item #143         5 story points     done
   Item #81         22 story points     done
   Item #209         8 story points     done
   Item #44         10 story points     ----
   Item #5           4 story points     ----
   Item #99         12 story points     ----

Iteration #2
   Item #44          8 story points     done
   Item #99         12 story points     done
   Item #163        14 story points     done
   Item #164         2 story points     done
   Item #166         5 story points     done
   Item #220         9 story points     ----
```

Items #44, #5, and #99 were sent back to the main list (e.g., the Product Backlog in the case of Scrum) and reordered. Item #5 was not on the top of the list anymore and so didn't find its way to the second iteration. Item #4 was re-estimated and its new size is 8 story points instead of 10.

Based on these values, our total output for done items is 86 story points ((10+5+22+8)+(8+12+14+2+5)) over two iterations, which makes our velocity 43 story points per iteration.

Take this scenario: An item was 10 story points, and you took it half-way in one iteration. It went back to the main list and was re-estimated to be 6 story points. It was finished in the next iteration. With the calculations explained above, the 4 story points that were worked on in the first iteration are lost and would not be included in our velocity. This is an accepted approximation because a similar thing may happen in every iteration and there will be a balance overall.

4.4.4.6 Abnormalities in velocity

Let's say our cumulative output for iterations has been as follows:

```
Iteration #1        45 story points
Iteration #2        41 story points
Iteration #3        49 story points
Iteration #4        52 story points
Iteration #5        178 story points
Iteration #6        55 story points
Iteration #7        58 story points
```

What's our velocity?

We can say that our total output is 478 story points in 7 iterations, which makes our velocity 68 story points per iteration (478÷7). This calculation is fine, but iteration #5 seems abnormal. The high value in that iteration may be justifiable, or unjustifiable. For example, maybe there was one item that had a high estimated value that turned out to be very simple, and we don't expect such exaggerated cases in the future. In this case, you can exclude iteration #7 from the velocity calculation, so, your total would be 300 story points in 6 iterations, equal to a velocity of 50 story points per iteration (300÷6).

In general, don't worry too much about calculating velocity and remember that it's a rough evaluation of speed for the two purposes of approximate planning and forecasting.

4.4.4.7 Starting velocity

As discussed in the previous chapters, we don't want to spend a separate period at the beginning of the project (e.g., Sprint zero) preparing for the project, but any preparation will be done gradually, alongside the normal development work of iterations. Because of this, and also because we may need some time to learn how to interact with each other and the customer, it's natural to have a low velocity at the beginning. It usually stabilizes after a few iterations, and after that, we can expect a small, steady increase because of our continuous improvements.

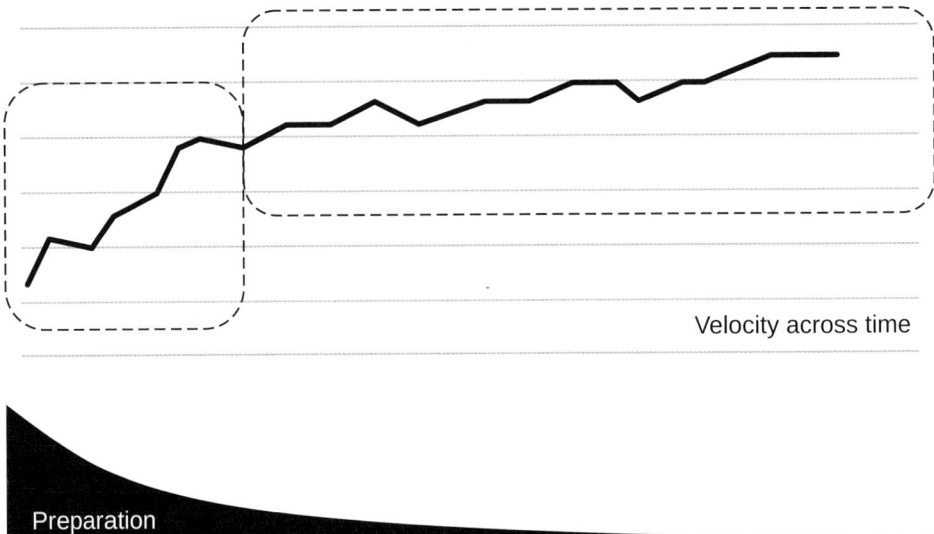

Velocity across time

Preparation

4.4.5 Planning poker

Regardless of which unit you use for measuring size, it's always the responsibility of the developers to estimate it. How can they do that?

The person responsible for composing the items (e.g., the Product Owner in Scrum) explains the items to the developers and asks them for the estimate. The developers discuss it with each other and then announce the estimate.

4.4.5.1 Biased estimation

It's best to have all developers involved in estimating and to use some form of voting. An overly simplified way of voting is to go through the developers, one at a time, and ask their opinions. Each developer gives their opinion, and when we have all the votes in, we can take the average as the team's opinion.

There is an issue with this method: The first few votes will anchor all the other opinions. For example, let's say there are 7 developers, and you're developer #4. You're thinking that the item is 3 to 7 story points, but you're not sure yet.

While you're thinking, people start voting from your right-hand side. When it's your turn, there's a good chance you would say 3 story points.

However, imagine the same scenario, but this time we vote from your left side. This time, there's a good chance you would say 7 story points.

The same phenomenon applies to most people in the team, and as a result, something arbitrary like the direction of voting can change the final result.

4.4.5.2 Unbiased estimation

In order to solve this issue, we should eliminate the possibility of anchoring. For example, each developer can write down their vote, and when they are all ready, they can show their votes.

This is a common way of estimating. When used in Agile projects, there's a special version of it called **planning poker**, in which developers have cards with numbers on them. Each one selects their card and keeps it face down until everyone is ready, and then they all show the cards together.

4.4.5.3 Voting again!

When all the cards are shown, we can check the deviation among the votes. If they are more or less in the same range, we can calculate an approximate average, and we'll be done. However, if the votes differ significantly, it probably means that some developers don't have a correct understanding of the work. In this case, it's a good idea to discuss the item once more and vote again. Remember, though, that some deviation is always to be expected, and that's what makes voting more effective.

4.4.5.4 Maximum or average

When all votes are ready, some teams take the maximum vote instead of the average as the final result, which is not a good idea. Taking the maximum value practically ignore all the votes except for one, which makes all the values less reliable. The average value is the most reliable one because it includes the considerations of all team members, and the noise in their estimates will more or less cancel out among them, while the single maximum value doesn't show such behavior.

The maximum value is usually used in environments where many Agile concepts are violated and developers are held accountable for delivering all the items planned for the iteration (which is absolutely wrong). In those environments, to make sure that no developer can say that the item's estimate was too optimistic and that's why they couldn't deliver it, they take the maximum value.

4.4.5.5 Planning poker cards

When using cards for planning poker, it's a good idea to limit the number of cards, because you don't want to hold a deck of cards with numbers from 1 to 200 (or something like that) and have to keep searching for the number you need. On the other hand, is there really a difference between 33 and 34 story points? Not at all.

To simplify the estimating process, there's a limited set of numbers available on the cards, with differences that make sense when it comes to estimating. A set of logarithmic values can be suitable for this purpose. Another good option that also matches many of the natural phenomena is the Fibonacci sequence, where each number is the sum of two previous numbers: 0, 1, 1, 2, 3, 5, 8, 13, 21, 34, etc.

The traditional planning poker cards use an adjusted Fibonacci sequence with some numbers rounded.

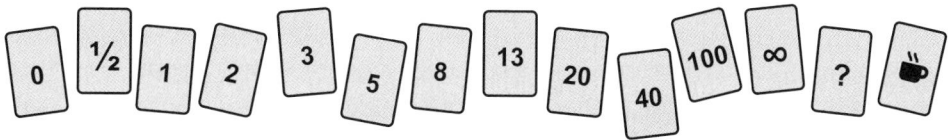

This is what some of the special cards in this deck mean:
- **0**: The item is too simple to spend time estimating it! It's almost nothing.
- **½**: Nothing says that story points can't have fractions. If the story is smaller than the reference, but it's not small enough to get a zero, you can give it half a story point.
- **?**: This means that you have no idea how much work it will take.
- **∞**: This item is just huge! We need to break it down into smaller items.
- ☕: This means that you're too tired and can't continue estimating anymore!

4.4.6 Triangulation

When we compare the stories with the reference and assign story points to them, we expect them to be comparable with each other. For example, if story A is 5 story points and story B is 10 story points, we expect B to take about twice as much effort as A to complete.

No estimation is perfect, and sometimes you might find that the estimated values are incompatible. To fix this issue, you can double-check them by comparing pairs of actual user stories with each other and make adjustments accordingly.

Another way to improve the estimates is to have multiple reference user stories for different sizes and use all of them for estimating each user story. For example, you can have a reference for 1 story point and another reference for 10 story points. When you compare the target story with the first reference and say that it takes five times the effort (5 story points), you should also compare it with the second reference and see whether it takes half of its effort.

Most of these extra provisions for increasing the reliability of the estimates that involve comparing them with more than one user story are described as **triangulation**.

Another method that implies some form of triangulation is to use a board with columns for each story size and put the user story cards in different columns to identify their estimates. When doing so, you will automatically compare them with each other and make adjustments. If you feel an urge to call this board by a name, you can call it the **triangulation board**.

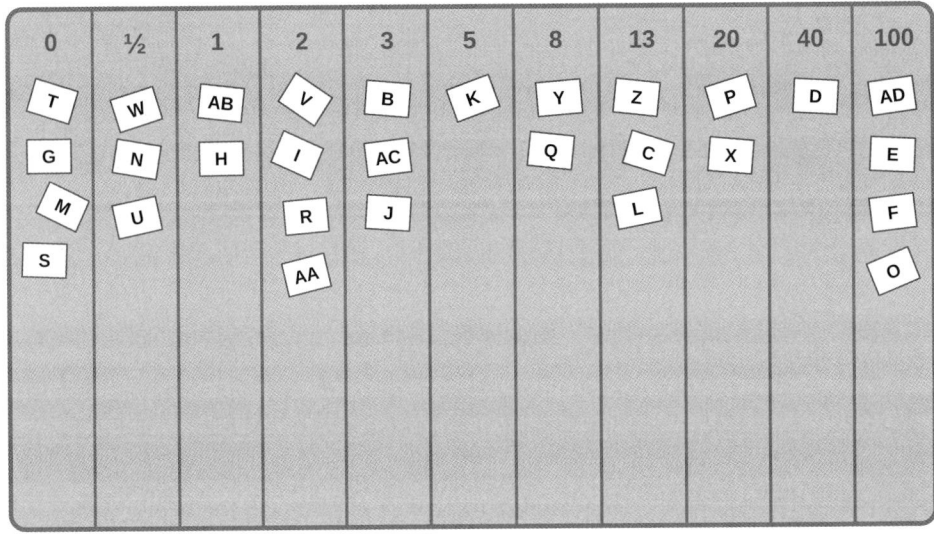

When triangulating, make sure you're not spending too much time on it and not aiming for an unnecessarily high level of accuracy.

4.4.7 Affinity estimation

Affinity estimation makes it easier to estimate multiple items at the same time, and it also implies some form of triangulation.

In this method, the story points are on cards, and you start by sorting them based on their relative size; e.g., from the smallest on the left to largest on the right-hand side of the board.

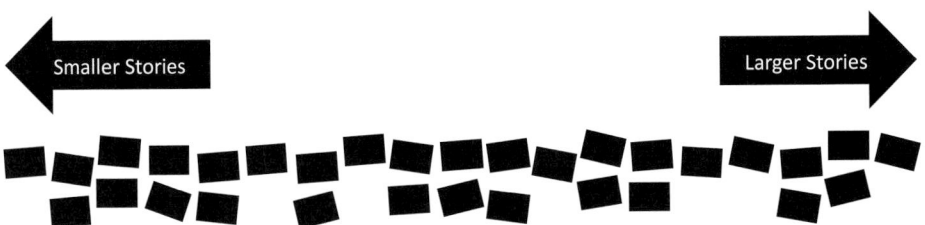

When you're done with sorting the items, you put them into a few groups that reflect their size.

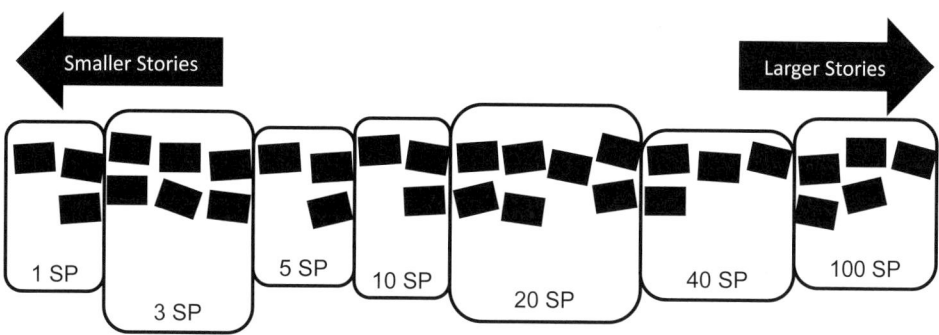

4.4.8 Re-estimating

Estimates are not written in stone, and we can re-estimate them to fix our previous misunderstandings or to reflect our newly increased knowledge of the project. However, we should remember that all the project environment's impact on performance is reflected in the velocity calculations, so we don't need to apply them to the estimation. For example, if we understand that the customer is not as collaborative as expected, we don't need to apply this to the estimates. Most of the estimation errors are fixed by the velocity calculations.

Estimates are just about the size of the items, and therefore, they should be revised only when we need to revise our opinion about the size of items, and not for other reasons such as our opinion about the amount of time it would take to develop the item.

4.5 Feedback loops

Feedback is everything in Agile! That's how we adapt.

There are different feedback loops, each with a different scope and a different possible outcome. XP demonstrates it as follows:[1]

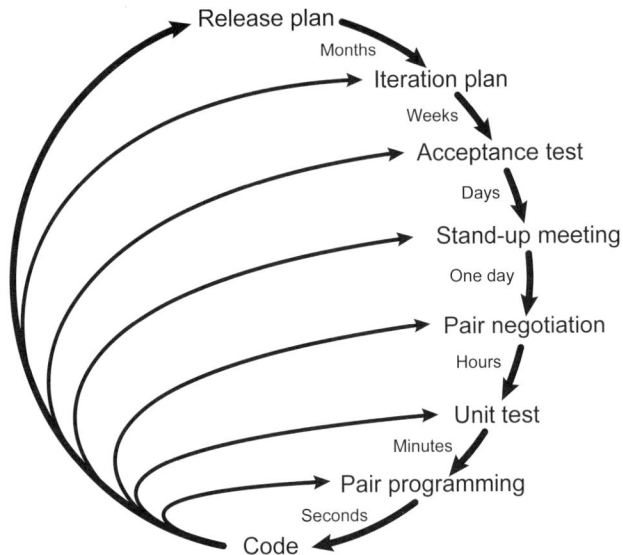

These are the loops, from small to large:
1. **Pair programming:** When pair programming, you may receive feedback from your peer every few seconds.
2. **Unit test:** Assuming that you're using test-driven development, you will be running the tests every few minutes to see if your latest additions to the code can pass the tests.
3. **Pair negotiation:** Every few hours, you and your peer discuss the design, overall approach, engineering approach, and so on.
4. **Stand-up meeting:** Once a day, everyone in the team gets together to see what's happening in the project and to synchronize.
5. **Acceptance test:** After a day, or possibly more, when you're done with an item, you will run its acceptance test and receive the first non-technical, external feedback.
6. **Iteration:** Every few weeks, an iteration ends and it is time to have a review and receive serious non-technical feedback from the customer and end-user representatives.
7. **Release:** Hopefully, you will have releases every few months, in which case, it will provide you with the best feedback of all: feedback from the real users.

All the above are necessary for achieving an optimum result, and practitioners have to pay attention and make sure they benefit from all (or at least most) of these.

---
1 CC BY-SA 3.0, https://en.wikipedia.org/wiki/Extreme_programming#/media/File:Extreme_Programming.svg

4.6 The Planning Onion

There are different levels of planning in an Agile project, and these can be shown in an onion-shaped diagram such as the one below:

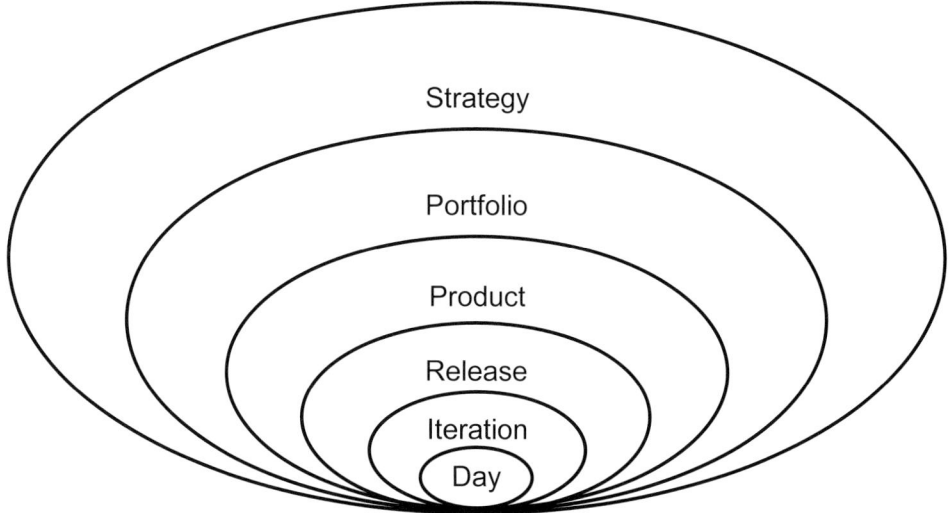

The strategy and portfolio planning levels are outside the projects, handled by the broader management systems of the organization. Strategy planning defines the benefits for the organization, and the portfolio level selects and resources the best possible projects to optimize the benefits.

Inside each Agile project, there are four conceptual levels of planning:

1. **Product planning:** This is a combination of the high-level vision for the product (e.g., Scrum's Product Goal) and the set of stories defined for the product (e.g., Scrum's Product Backlog).
2. **Release planning:** Scrum doesn't have a release management system built in, but Scrum projects can add it themselves. Other systems such as XP, Crystal, and DSDM have their own approaches to release management that define when and how the increments will be released to production.
3. **Iteration planning:** This level is about planning iterations one at a time; e.g., Scrum's Sprint Planning.
4. **Day planning:** The stand-up meeting (Scrum's Daily Scrum) is about daily planning.

5. DSDM®

Does Agile allow project managers?

Many people say no, because Agile is the same as Scrum to them. Scrum does not allow project managers, but that's just Scrum, and it doesn't have to be the same as that in every system. DSDM is an Agile methodology, as old as XP, Crystal, and Scrum. DSDM has a project manager role, a comprehensive process, and many artifacts. Unlike Scrum, though, which is primarily created for small projects with just one team, DSDM supports multiple teams and is suitable for larger projects by default.

In this chapter, we're going to review a few aspects of DSDM that will help you understand the range of possibilities in Agile.

5.1 Project Constraints

Are you familiar with the classical project constraints triangle?

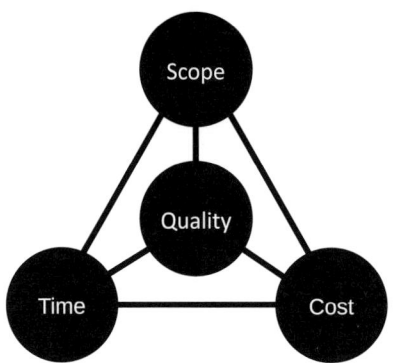

Scope, time, cost, and quality are the primary constraints in projects, and they are shown like this because of the relationship they have with each other: To change one of them, you usually have to change at least one other constraint to balance the triangle. For example, to deliver the project sooner, you might have to spend more money, remove some elements from the scope, lower the quality, or any combination of these.

Each of these four elements can be fixed or dynamic. Logically, we always need to have at least one dynamic element among these four, otherwise it won't be possible to balance the constraints. In most predictive projects, the scope is fixed, and the rest have targets but are dynamic. It's usually desirable to fix quality as well. Take a construction project: What happens if you're behind schedule? Would you say that time is fixed and you have to deliver the project without windows and utilities, or do you extend the time and complete the scope? The nature of this project dictates a fixed scope.

Now, let's say you're building a complex for the Olympic Games. How would you see the constraints in this project? Time is absolutely fixed. Because of the type of project, the scope is almost fixed (at least partially). You don't want to compromise quality because that would be very bad for the reputation of the country. What remains then? Just cost. So, if you want to fix scope, quality, and time, you should be really dynamic about cost!

DSDM claims that the traditional way of fixing scope is not effective because of the following reasons:
- It causes the project to be delivered later. This is undesirable because software products have a very short lifespan, and when delivered later, they have a shorter life in production and so generate less benefit.

- It causes everyone to add too many unnecessary features that will never be used to the product, and these increase the cost of the project as well as the maintenance cost of the product.

So, DSDM keeps the scope dynamic, and instead fixes time, cost, and quality[2]:

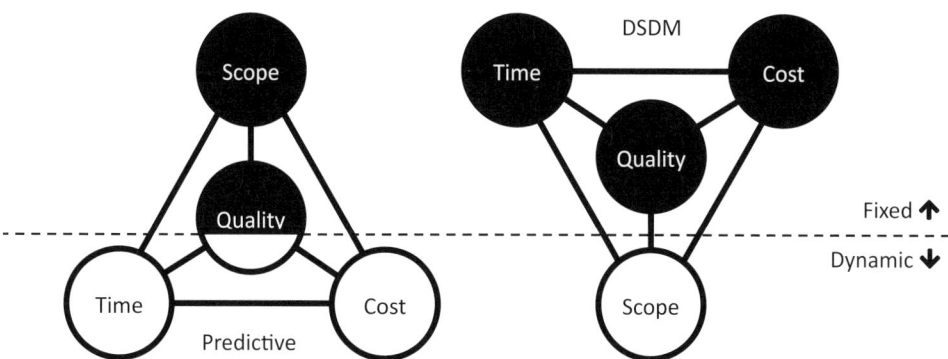

Keeping the scope dynamic is common among all Agile systems because they are adaptive, and therefore, we don't know the whole scope upfront to fix it. However, fixing time for the whole project is a special characteristic of DSDM that doesn't exist in all systems.

A typical Scrum project may continue until the customer decides that the product is mature and valuable enough. A DSDM project, on the other hand, is finished exactly on time, not even 1 day later (the timeboxing concept), and we deliver as much as possible in this period. Then, if the customer decides to, they can start another timeboxed DSDM project to add more features to the same product. In this sense, DSDM doesn't force you to stop working on the product but rather forces you to pause and see it as an important decision.

So, let's say you have an external customer and you have to decide on the timeboxed duration of the project (and cost). How would you do that? We'll talk about that next.

5.2 Upfront Planning

Is it fine to have upfront planning in Agile?

Yes, there's nothing wrong with it, as long as it's a high-level plan that doesn't block adaptation. What's not suitable for Agile is detailed upfront planning.

---

2 Based on a similar diagram from DSDM manual:
   https://www.agilebusiness.org/page/ProjectFramework_03_PhilosophyFundamentals

We can consider two approaches:
- **No plan upfront:** We just carry on with the project and let the whole scope emerge during the project. This is the default approach in Scrum.
- **Enough plan upfront:** This is the DSDM approach in which we create a high-level plan upfront and use adaptation for the details of each feature. For example, we make an upfront decision that we need to have a minimal customer relationship management (CRM) system on our website. But, what features are we going to have in the CRM system? That's what we leave to emerge during the project with our adaptive approach.

As you can imagine, the DSDM approach to project constraints requires a high-level upfront plan to be prepared and then used as the basis for setting the duration and cost of the project.

Let's say we have the high-level plan; how can we set time and cost when we don't know the details? We'll talk about that next.

5.3 MoSCoW Prioritization

The MoSCoW prioritization is a great technique for scope management, and it's an essential part of DSDM. Its use is not even limited to Agile methods and generic methods such as PRINCE2® use it as well.

MoSCoW is a combination of the first letters of must-have, should-have, could-have, and won't-have-this-time. In this technique, we assign one of those priorities to each feature, based on the following definitions:
- **Must-have:** A must-have feature is one that must be in the final product, as the final product would be useless without it (e.g., brakes in a car).
- **Should-have:** A should-have feature is an important feature of the final product, and we will face problems without it. However, we can find a workaround for the problems and it's still possible to use the solution without it (e.g., air conditioning in a car).
- **Could-have:** A could-have feature is a helpful feature that we would like to have in our solution, but it would not create a problem if we didn't have it (e.g., a rear camera for reversing in a car).
- **Won't-have-this-time:** A won't-have feature may be interesting, but we're not going to invest in it now.

In a setup like this, we can think of these possibilities:
- The **minimum** for an acceptable product is the solution that contains all the must-have features.

- Our **expected** product is the one that contains all the must-have and should-have items.
- The **ideal** product is the one that contains all the must-have, should-have, and could-have items.

MoSCoW prioritization is a great way to focus on the business value – focusing on the real needs instead of the fancy extra features (could-have items).

Going back to the question of setting the time and cost of the project based on a high-level upfront plan, we assign MoSCoW priorities to all features. Then, we need to come up with a duration that is long enough for developing all the must-have items with pessimistic estimates, and also long enough to develop everything in the project with an optimistic estimate. This would be the timeboxed duration of the project.

The rule is that must-have items should be less than 60% of all items, and could-have items should be at least 20% of all items. This helps with the logic behind the methodology.

5.4 Exceptions

How would you measure progress in a DSDM project?

An important metric in most projects is the forecast for the completion time and cost, but these are fixed in DSDM.

As you can imagine, what we do is forecast the project constraints that are dynamic, which in the case of DSDM is the scope. We will be forecasting the items we can deliver by the end of the project, and if, at any time, we forecast that we cannot deliver all the must-have items by the end of the project, we will have an **exception**. The issue would then be escalated to the higher levels of management to check alternatives and make a decision.

Pure Scrum practitioners may be unfamiliar with the escalation concept. In your opinion, does it work against the self-organization of the team?

5.5 Self-Organization

In DSDM, some decisions are made by higher level managers rather than the normal team members. We saw one example just before this. Another example is that items we pick for the **development timeboxes** (iterations are called development timeboxes in DSDM) have local MoSCoW priorities that relate to the project-level MoSCoW priorities but are different. If there's an issue about a could-have item within the timebox, the team members will decide how to deal with it, but if it's about a should-have or a must-have item, they will escalate the issue.

So, as you see, the authority of the local team is limited. The fact is that no Agile team has absolute power, as it's always limited by the method/framework, as well as other constraints such as organizational rules. For example, a Scrum team is self-organized, but they cannot decide to extend their Sprints because Sprints are timeboxed in the Scrum framework. So, self-organization is just a relative label we use when the authority of the team is higher than a certain level. What level is that? There's no definition.

5.6 Contract Types

Most customers want to have **fixed-price** contracts because they believe they are safer, which is not correct. What do you think about having a fixed-price contract in an Agile project?

Well, you've already seen that DSDM projects have a fixed duration and a fixed cost, so, it would be fine to have a fixed-price contract. However, the type of fixed-price contract in DSDM is not what most people have in mind. In DSDM, it's a **fixed-price, dynamic-scope** contract, whereas what people are looking for is a **fixed-price, fixed-scope** contract.

Some customers will force a fixed-price, fixed-scope contract that is based on a detailed, upfront definition of scope. However, this is simply incompatible with Agile because there's no room for adaptation when the scope is defined in detail. You can never fix this fundamental problem with minor considerations nor with any adjustments to your approach without destroying its adaptive nature. However, since many suppliers face this problem, there are a few approaches to managing fixed-price, fixed-scope contracts. They generally try to convert the contract from a real fixed-price contract into a time-and-material or fixed-unit one, while the fixed-price name is kept to make the customer happy. Along the way, they may sacrifice some level of Agility also. For example, one rather common approach is to define the items upfront (not Agile enough), and then when the customer asks for a new item, ask them to swap it with one or a few existing items of the same size.

The best option for most Agile projects, such as Scrum projects, is time-and-material, where the customer simply pays the supplier a certain amount for each developer-hour spent on the project, or any variation of that, such as a certain amount for each Sprint, when the duration of the Sprint and the number of developers involved in the project are fixed.

6. Kanban

Kanban is a technique originally used in manufacturing. It has been recently used in IT projects as well, either as an additional technique alongside Scrum or as a stand-alone system. The standalone system differs from all Agile systems in that it doesn't have timeboxed iterations, and instead, uses a continuous flow where items are picked from a backlog (similar to Scrum's Product Backlog) whenever there's free capacity. Regardless of the lack of iterations, it still has iterative development and incremental delivery, and when done right, it can be considered a proper adaptive system.

The following are some of the key attributes of Kanban:
1. Work should be visualized.
2. Work in progress (WIP) should be limited.
3. Work should be pulled instead of pushed.

Let's see what these three attributes mean.

6.1 Visualizing

Visualizing is really helpful because
- it creates transparency, and therefore, improves feedback and collaboration;
- it provides better control over the process.

We prepare a **Kanban board** to visualize the work steps and the work items. The steps depend on the type of work and the preferences of the team. An example can be steps such as *to do*, *designing*, *programming*, *testing*, *documenting*, and *done*, as shown in the next image.

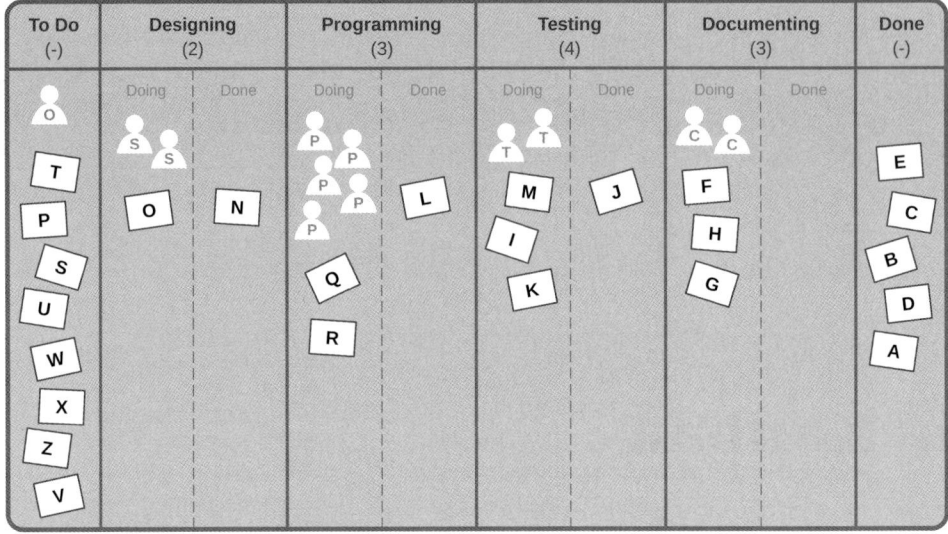

This is what we mean by **visualizing** in this context.

6.2 Limiting WIP

Having too many unfinished work items is not a good idea because it's distracting and switching between them wastes a lot of energy. It's best to limit the WIP, and focus on finishing items before moving to the next ones.

Limiting WIP is helpful in every type of project, and probably in every type of work in general. For example, the concept of Sprints and Sprint Backlogs in Scrum is a form of limiting WIP because instead of having access to an unlimited number of items from the Product Backlog, you constrain yourself to the limited set available in the Sprint Backlog. However, the Sprint Backlog is not a big limit for WIP, and it's useful for Scrum teams to limit their WIP beyond the limits of their Sprint Backlogs.

When it comes to Kanban, WIP has an essential role. The whole Kanban technique is based on limiting WIP and using a pull system, and therefore, we can't call something Kanban if WIP is not limited. For example, calling task boards such as those in Trello "Kanban boards" is not correct.

To get a better visualization, it's a good idea to write the WIP limits on the Kanban board, as you can see in the previous image. In that example, we've decided not to program more than 3 items at the same time. The proper limit depends on the number of people available for the process and the nature of the work, and it usually takes trial and error to find the optimum limit.

6.3 Pull vs. Push

Check the previous image once again. Except for the first and last columns, each column has two sub columns: one for the items that are being processed in that column, and the second for those that are completed in that step. The important point here is that items in both columns are counted as WIP for that step. This is so because we have a pull system in Kanban, which means that we can't push the completed work to the next step, but we have to wait for them to pull it into their step when they have free capacity. Based on this definition, you can see that all columns are at full capacity in the previous image, and none of them can pull a new work item to their column.

Now, let's say the documenting team is done with item G. This initiates a number of moves on the board:

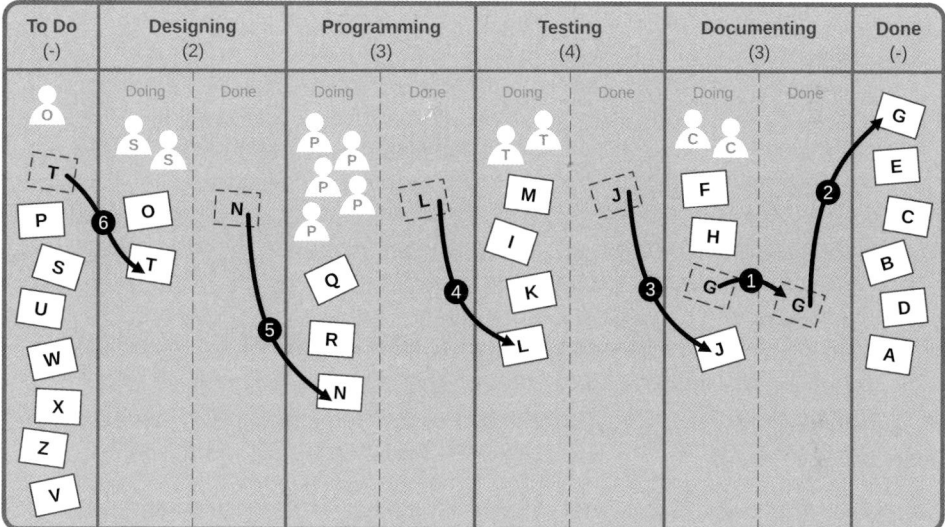

This is what happens in order:
1. G is done, and therefore, it goes to the second sub column of the *documenting* column.
2. Since *documenting* is the last working step, G will automatically go to the *done* column.
3. Now there are only two items in the *documenting* column (items F and H), which means there's one unit of free capacity in this column. People in this column can pull item J from the previous column, since it was marked as done with *testing*.
4. Now that J is out of *testing*, there are only three items in the *testing* column (items M, I, and K), and since its WIP limit is 4, they can pull in item L from the previous column, which was marked as done for *programming*.
5. Again, there is an open space in the *programming* column, so they can pull in the item N, which was marked as done with *designing*.

6. Now the designers also have a free capacity, so they can pull in a new item from the *to do* column (item T).

Note that all items in the *to do* column should be sorted based on whatever criterion suits our environment (e.g., value), and therefore, we always pick the top most item in this column.

This is the current state:

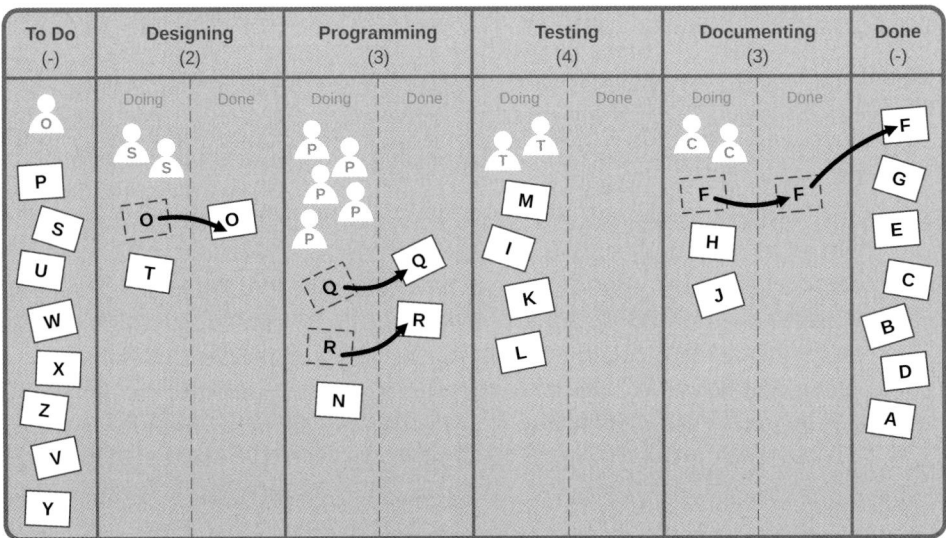

After a while, some items in each column are completed and are moved to the sub-column to their right:

Check the previous image and see what changes we can make. What do you think? Can we move any of the items? No. We cannot have any moves on the board at this moment. There's one free capacity unit in *documenting*, but no item is ready in the previous column. In the *programming* column, there's only one unfinished item, but as you remember, we also have to count the items in the sub-column to the right, which means that there's no free capacity in *programming*. The same applies to the *designing* column.

After a while, the designers are done with item T:

So, what can happen now? Designers don't have anything else to do and, since this is a pull system, they can't push their finished items to the next column to free up room for a new item. In this case, the designers can move to another column and help their colleagues. Which column, though? The bottleneck is in *testing*:

This can be the case for everyone in the team. For example, the remaining items in *programming* and *documenting* can be done as well, before *testing* finishes anything else.

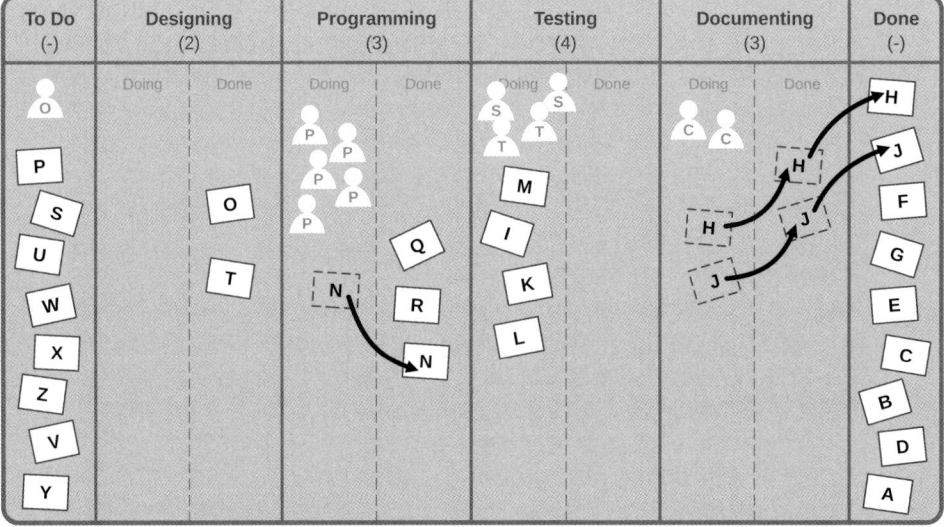

At this point, all the columns are full to capacity, and their members also have to move to the *testing* column. Even the person in the *to do* column, who you can think of as a Product Owner, should move to the *testing* column, since it doesn't matter what items that person puts in the column as they're not going to be developed yet.

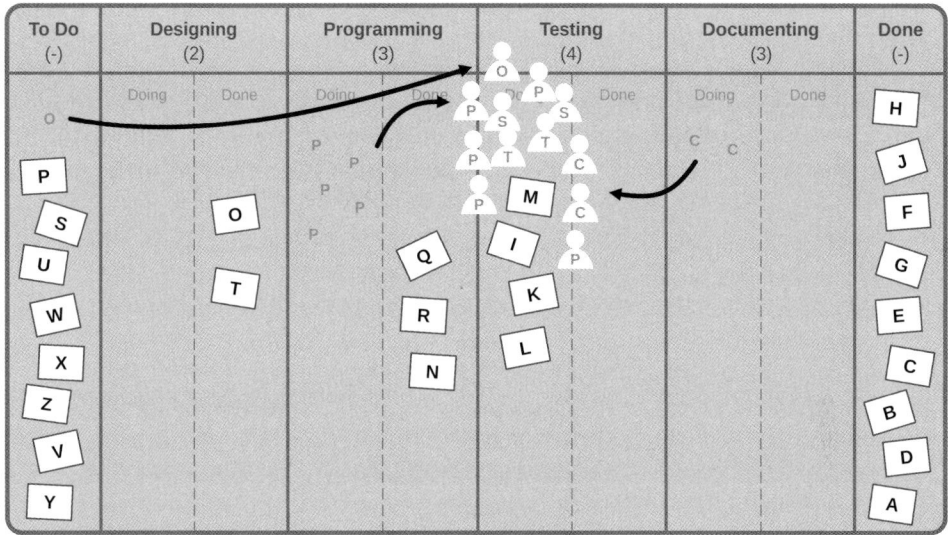

So, everyone works in the *testing* column until we have the first item complete in that column and have the flow of the process back to normal. Now everyone goes back to their original columns and focuses on their own specialty again.

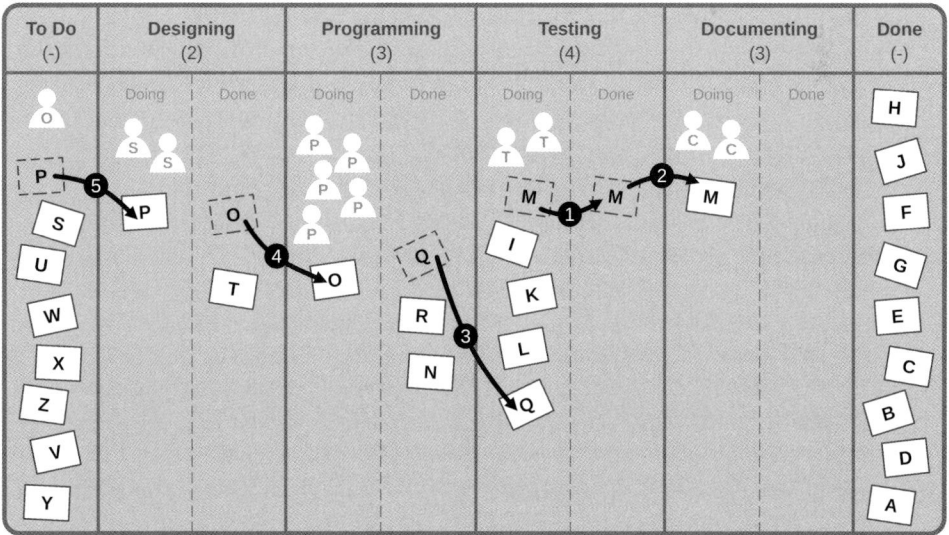

The scenario above shows what it means to have a pull system with a WIP limit. In such a system, everyone involved in the process is focused on the flow of items, and on getting things done instead of being only focused on their specialist activities. This may seem strange to expect someone not to start working on a new item and instead try to help people in an area they are not expert in, but in practice, it helps create a more productive environment.

On the other hand, every once in a while when people have to stop working on their columns and move somewhere else to help, they learn more about the rest of the process, which will be helpful to them in their own specialist activities when they return.

7. Philosophizing!

Various people and systems have presented the Agile concept in different ways, each with an emphasis on the common problems of their time and environment. We'll explore a few of them, and follow with the Agile Manifesto, which is the collective work of people who pioneered Agile in 2001. While the unifying and simplifying nature of the manifesto is attractive, it's important to have diversity and openness, and that's the reason for navigating the ideas from various systems in this section.

7.1 eXtreme Programming Ideas

eXtreme Programming (XP) used to be the dominant Agile method in the beginning, mainly because of its solid, integrated set of practices, which makes it very practical.

Besides the integrated set of practices, which was explored in the eXtreme Programming chapter, it also had high-level ideas about how projects should work. These ideas are mainly, but not entirely, represented in two bills of rights and a set of values.

7.1.1 Customer bill of rights

A successful project needs a positive, effective relationship between the customer and the supplier. To have a constant reminder of the rights we afford to the customer, the customer's bill of rights is prepared in XP. This outline of customer rights makes our relationship clearer and gives us (as the supplier) a strategy to have in mind all the time.

The most important thing to remember about the customer-supplier relationship is that they are not competing entities, but they should consider each other as parts of the same team, with the same goal of creating a valuable product.

7.1.1.1 Overall plan

> As the customer, you have the right to an overall plan, to know what can be accomplished when and at what cost.

Agile systems replace the plan-driven, predictive approach with an adaptive one. Naturally, we don't have as much planning in Agile as we have in a predictive system, but it doesn't mean that we don't have any type of planning. Since there is a common misconception in the Agile community that once you start using Agile you can or should say goodbye to all types of planning, XP and DSDM have a special emphasis on the necessity of having a plan. What type of plan, though? We need to have a high-level, overall plan for the project.

This type of planning is necessary because projects are not run in isolation but are parts of bigger portfolios and only make sense in the context of the overall business. To make sure there's enough alignment, we need to have a high-level plan, and make it compatible with the rest of the business.

7.1.1.2 The most value

> As the customer, you have the right to get the most possible value out of every programming week.

There are two aspects to this right:
- We need to be thinking about generating value. While this may sound simple, there's a difference between being focused on doing certain works and letting them generate value, and being focused on generating value and checking to see what we have to do to achieve this. It's all about perspective.
- At any time, we need to be working on features that generate the most value instead of any other set of features.

This concept is one of the most common ones among all Agile systems.

7.1.1.3 Progress

> As the customer, you have the right to see progress in a running system, proven to work by passing repeatable tests that you specify.

Agile is about adaptation, and this adaptation is based on the feedback generated by a piece of **working software** rather than abstract, unfinished code. This is so because only complete, ready, usable, and releasable code can generate reliable feedback. Any code that is not completely done is a source of surprises for the future and a potential block.

7.1.1.4 Change

> As the customer, you have the right to change your mind, to substitute functionality, and to change priorities without paying exorbitant costs.

The main reason we use an adaptive system is that in this type of project we can't rely on an upfront specification of the product. We use a system that is not based on a prediction of the future or an upfront plan and design. Therefore, our customers don't have to come up with all their requirements at the beginning, and they can always change their minds during the project.

7.1.1.5 Schedule

> As the customer, you have the right to be informed of schedule changes, in time to choose how to reduce the scope to restore the original date. You can cancel at any time and be left with a useful working system reflecting investment to date.

In a proper adaptive system, each work item is completely finished before we set it aside and start working on something else. This means that all types of tests (unit testing, regression testing, user acceptance testing, etc.) are done for the item. As a result, our increments are completely releasable, and we can stop the project at any time and have a working piece of software left.

This is a great advantage because when we focus on value and work for the most valuable items at any time, the most important parts of the software will be developed early in the project, and as time passes, the potential for generating value decreases. After a while, the customer may see that even though they still have lots of items in the backlog, they won't be able to contribute enough value and so it's time to stop the project.

7.1.2 Programmer bill of rights

Customers have certain rights; after all, they are the ones paying for the project. However, the suppliers (programmers) have rights as well, and the customer should recognize these to create an effective environment.

XP was formed a long time ago, when the development environment was simpler than today, and as a result, it always refers to "programmers". Nowadays, we use the term "developer", which is more inclusive and includes programmers as well as testers, architects, UI designers, analysts, etc.

7.1.2.1 Priorities

> As a programmer, you have the right to know what is needed, with clear declarations of priority.

We don't need a complete upfront plan, but we still need to know the requirements at some point and have an understanding of their priorities to enable them to focus on and generate value. This becomes harder when there are multiple people or departments from the customer side involved in specifying the needs because they usually have contradictory expectations. There has to be a system in place to deal with this difficulty, and the customer should support it regardless.

7.1.2.2 Quality

> As a programmer, you have the right to produce quality work at all times.

In most projects, quality is considered the customer's right. However, in programming, quality is also the programmers' right. A good programmer knows that quality code takes longer to build, but saves them a lot more time and trouble in the future. As a result, they do want to produce quality code. However, sometimes, others force them to deliver something as soon as possible, before ensuring that the code has their desired level of quality. This is the programmers' right to take their time and bring any new piece of code to the level of quality that satisfies themselves before moving on to the next work item.

7.1.2.3 Help

> As a programmer, you have the right to ask for and receive help.

Let's say you're working on a part of the application that receives personal information from users, and you have doubts about the way it should be implemented to comply with GDPR. You shouldn't be worried about asking for such help.

7.1.2.4 Estimates

> As a programmer, you have the right to make and update your own estimates.

We need to let people who will do the work estimate it, rather than having a manager estimate the work and force those unrealistic estimates on the team.

7.1.2.5 Empowerment

> As a programmer, you have the right to accept your responsibilities instead of having them assigned to you.

Nowadays, this is usually called self-organization. While it's not mandatory for having an adaptive system, most of the original Agile systems were created for small teams, whereas having empowered teams could be advantageous.

7.1.3 Values

There are five values behind XP, and having them in mind makes the adoption of XP more effective. These are not mandatory values in every Agile system, but very common among all of them.

7.1.3.1 Communication

Lack of effective communication is a common source of problems in projects. This is so important that both the PMBOK® Guide (a famous standard and guide about project management, leaning toward predictive systems) and PRINCE2® (a general project management methodology, compatible with both methods, but closer to predictive systems) state that project managers need to spend 80 to 90% of their time on communications. They also have many artifacts and processes for improving communications.

The same applies to Agile projects: We need to take communications seriously. This includes conversations as well as passive forms of communication such as information radiators.

7.1.3.2 Simplicity

When more requirements are received, it may seem natural to satisfy them by adding more features on top of each other. However, that makes for a complicated solution that is hard to maintain and extend. The best way is to keep the software as simple as possible and try to find creative ways of satisfying the requirements.

Sometimes a requirement may have the potential to add some value to the product, but the amount of value is not enough to justify the complexities it introduces to the system. In these cases, it's best to have a conversation with the customer and convince them to ignore such requirements.

7.1.3.3 Feedback
Feedback is essential to adaptive systems. We create increments of the product and let the customer and end-user representatives work with them, and generate feedback. That feedback is what we use to find our way and adapt.

We also like to have releases whenever possible, because when the application is released, real end-users will be using it and so we will have more reliable feedback for the system.

7.1.3.4 Courage
We do have certain fears; for example, you've been working on something for a while, and just before finishing it, you can think of a better way of doing it that could be helpful in the future. You need to have the courage to change it. Sometimes, you may be able to think of a novel solution to a problem, which seems promising but also dangerous because no one else is doing that. You need to have the courage to try it within reason.

7.1.3.5 Respect
We rely on having a highly collaborative environment, and for this to happen, we need to respect each other.

7.2 DSDM® Ideas

DSDM is different from other first-generation Agile systems in that it was originally created for larger projects with multiple teams. Let's have a look at its "philosophy" (as they call it) and set of principles to understand their perspective.

7.2.1 Philosophy

> Best business value emerges when projects are aligned to clear business goals, deliver frequently and involve the collaboration of motivated and empowered people.

This statement implies that the ultimate goal is to generate **business value**, and in order to do so, the following considerations are essential:
- **Have a clear business goal.** Value is a subjective concept, meaning that what is valuable for one person may not be valuable for another. So, we want to be focused on generating value, but what is valuable for the customer and end-users? The business goal and our organizational strategies answer this question. You can interpret this item as "Before focusing on creating value, define what is valuable for you."

- **Deliver frequently.** This is about having iterative development and incremental delivery, which are required for making sure that our assumptions about value were correct, and if not, realigning ourselves before it's too late.
- **Create a collaborative environment.** There's always collaboration in every project, but what we usually mean by collaboration in Agile, is the collaboration between the customer and the supplier, working in a one-team culture.
- **Motivate and empower people.** Empowering project team members by having a proper level of delegation is always a necessity in projects (both adaptive and predictive), and so important that it's one of the principles in PRINCE2 as well. It has multiple positive consequences, and one of them is that people will be more motivated. When it comes to empowerment, however, note that a small project (a typical XP or Scrum project) can engender almost absolute empowerment, but as we move to larger projects such as those targeted in DSDM and PRINCE2, there will be more limits to empowerment.

7.2.2 Principles

DSDM was highly influenced by one of the most well-formed project management methods of its time, PRINCE2. Following the same structure as PRINCE2, they have introduced a number of principles that should be considered in everything you do in a DSDM project.

7.2.2.1 Focus on the business need

You may be asking yourself what the ultimate goal is: to generate value or to satisfy the business need? The fact is that these two are tied together. Being focused on value carries the risk of forgetting about the subjective, relative nature of value, and mixing what is valuable for the customer and the end-user with what is valuable for yourself. This is why the more structured approaches to projects usually talk about business needs, business goals, and organizational strategies, as those are the elements behind what is valuable for the project.

Scrum, on the other hand, used to be entirely focused on value, and it was responsible for making value the center of attention for many people. However, even the 2020 edition of the Scrum Guide has distanced itself from this notion by introducing the concept of "product goal", and now, the Scrum Guide talks more about satisfying the product goal than generating business value.

7.2.2.2 Deliver on time

For many IT projects, time to market is essential, and a matter of winning or losing. However, there's no doubt that this is a combination of time and the features you have in your application. An application that is first in the market but doesn't satisfy the end-users won't be successful. Even worse, it may prepare the market for a competitor who will provide a satisfying solution in the same domain.

DSDM addresses both of these issues by having fixed-duration projects to ensure they are never late, and using MoSCoW prioritization to ensure that the final product will contain all the must-have items.

7.2.2.3 Collaborate

Instead of a customer-supplier categorization, DSDM is focused on the following categorization, which is a mixture of representatives from the customer side and the supplier side:
- Technical;
- Managerial;
- Business-oriented;
- Process-oriented.

These four categories represent all types of "interest" in the project and how different types of people contribute to the project. These people need to collaborate and work as one team with the same goal.

7.2.2.4 Never compromise quality

As discussed in XP's bill of rights for programmers, quality has two aspects: one that helps the customer achieve what they need, and one that helps the supplier maintain and extend the solution without running into dead ends. We don't want to compromise quality because that always causes problems sooner or later.

One advantage in adaptive systems when it comes to quality is that tests are not compressed towards the end of the project when we're running out of time and may have to cut corners. Instead, Agile projects have continuous testing, and as long as we have a disciplined way of working, quality won't be compromised.

7.2.2.5 Build incrementally from firm foundations

This principle has two aspects:
- **Build incrementally.** All adaptive systems have to use incremental delivery to enable reliable feedback.
- **Have a firm foundation for increments.** This aspect is different from some of the other Agile systems such as Scrum. The firm foundation referred to in the principle is an upfront high-level plan that helps us direct the project, while we adapt in a lower layer. It is certainly up to you to decide about the depth and width of this foundation and balance your level of adaptation with the desired level of prediction.

7.2.2.6 Develop iteratively

In order to have incremental delivery, we have to run the development processes iteratively. In other words, instead of designing everything once and then moving to the next process, we have to repeat the design process for individual features and develop iteratively.

7.2.2.7 Communicate continuously and clearly

This is, once again, the concern we have in all types of project: effective communications. What we expect from a system, though, is to go beyond advising the importance of something and give a practical solution that helps achieve it; and DSDM, like every other method, has its own approach to improving communications.

7.2.2.8 Demonstrate control

Some people think that planning, monitoring, and controlling is incompatible with Agility, but this is not correct. Every project needs these elements, but the way they are implemented may be different based on the development approach. What DSDM emphasizes is that because you're using an Agile approach doesn't mean that you don't need to control the project.

We first monitor the status of the project and determine where we are and where we will be towards the end, and then, if there are deviations, we control them by designing and implementing corrective and preventive actions.

A crucial consequence of having proper monitoring and controlling is that if the project becomes unjustifiable, we will know, and we can cancel the project without wasting more money on it. Remember that cancelling projects is a sign of good project management.

7.3 Scrum Ideas

Scrum may not have the same solid background and foundation as XP, Crystal, and DSDM, but it has also evolved in response to its wide adoption in recent years, and one of the recent changes in it was the introduction of Scrum values. In addition to that, Scrum considers three pillars for itself, which are more or less like principles.

7.3.1 Pillars

Scrum considers the following as its pillars:
- Transparency;
- Inspection;
- Adaptation.

However, these three are not at the same level. The most important one is **adaptation**, as no Scrum project can be considered Agile if it's not adaptive. On the other hand, in order to adapt, you need to evaluate your current state by **inspecting** the product and the way you work. Finally, in order to inspect, it really helps to be **transparent** and let all the stakeholders know the way of work, the progress, and the product, and give you their inputs on these.

7.3.2 Values
The values newly added to scrum are elements that internal and external stakeholders need to consider in order to become more efficient.

7.3.2.1 Commitment
There's been a lot of misunderstanding about the concept of commitment in Agile. Some people think that when the developers pick a number of items for an iteration, their primary commitment is to deliver all of them. This is a counterproductive notion that pushes the developers to be more conservative and pick fewer items, as no one wants to be blamed for not honoring their commitments, which in turn causes them to deliver fewer items. This is the case because work expands to fill in the available time (Parkinson's Law).

The real commitment in Scrum is to generate value, as it was in the past, or to achieve the product goal, as it is in recent versions.

7.3.2.2 Courage
Similarly to XP practitioners, Scrum users need to have the courage to do the right thing and face difficult problems.

7.3.2.3 Focus
You need to be focused on the goals and the generation of value rather than on the lines of code you have written, the speed of development (velocity), whether or not you have finished everything in the backlog, etc.

7.3.2.4 Openness
What's the point of having an adaptive system if we're not open to exploring various ideas for the product? However, openness is not limited to the product, and also covers the way we work. We need to be open to various practices (e.g., XP practices), and even other systems, including the well-established predictive systems.

Unfortunately, some of the "leaders" in the Agile community in general, and the Scrum community in particular, do not embrace this value and even discourage it with their actions. They do this by considering competing systems as enemies, even when they are not familiar enough with those systems.

7.3.2.5 Respect
This value is about respecting each other, and also respecting the resources we have for the project (e.g., our time and capacity).

7.4 The Agile Manifesto

Some people started using adaptive systems for IT development and gradually structured them into repeatable management processes. A group of these pioneers got together in 2001 to make it official by giving it a name and creating a manifesto.

This is the manifesto they created:

> We are uncovering better ways of developing software by doing it and helping others do it. Through this work we have come to value:
> - Individuals and interactions over processes and tools;
> - Working software over comprehensive documentation;
> - Customer collaboration over contract negotiation;
> - Responding to change over following a plan.
>
> That is, while there is value in the items on the right, we value the items on the left more.
>
> Kent Beck, Mike Beedle, Arie van Bennekum, Alistair Cockburn, Ward Cunningham, Martin Fowler, James Grenning, Jim Highsmith, Andrew Hunt, Ron Jeffries, Jon Kern, Brian Marick, Robert C. Martin, Steve Mellor, Ken Schwaber, Jeff Sutherland, Dave Thomas © 2001, the above authors. This declaration may be freely copied in any form, but only in its entirety through this notice.

It's a simple guide that hints at what they meant when they talked about Agile, but unfortunately, most people take it as the ultimate truth about Agile, which is not correct because this manifesto itself has never been subject to adaptation. Rather, it was created once by a limited number of people in response to their own environment, and stayed the same after that.

Let's review each of those four values next.

7.4.1 Statement #1

> We value individuals and interactions over processes and tools.

This statement addresses two common problems. The first problem is that some people think that tools can solve their problems; e.g., they can implement a sophisticated project management system and it will magically solve their problems in their projects. This is rarely, if ever, the case. What we need are **solutions**, and only after that might we want to see whether there are any tools to help with our solutions. Tools only facilitate solutions – they are not a substitute for them.

The second issue that is addressed in this statement is about individuals and their interactions. People are complicated, and when you bring many of them together to work on a project, numerous problems may surface. These problems have roots in human behavior, and there's only one way of dealing with them: paying attention to human behavior, finding the root causes, and trying to solve them. While this may sound simple, many managers try to solve the problem by reducing the impact of human interactions on the whole system (usually by designing a different system). This approach is theoretically valid, but in practice, it doesn't work well.

The manifesto values individuals and interactions over processes, but in reality, an important thing that Agile systems have done is to value individuals and interactions by the type of processes they have created – processes that put people at the center of the system.

So, in summary, processes that try to ignore or replace human aspects are ineffective, whereas processes that address those aspects and make them part of the system are desirable.

This statement applies to all projects regardless of their development approach.

7.4.2 Statement #2

> We value working software over comprehensive documentation.

In contrast to the previous statement, which applies to all types of projects, this one is specific to adaptive systems. It refers to the fact that instead of using upfront documentation to predict what needs to happen in a project, we just go on, create pieces of working software (increments), and use them to adapt. This is so because in this type of project the customer doesn't seem to know what they want until they see the product.

7.4.3 Statement #3

> We value customer collaboration over contract negotiation.

Any project will be more successful with higher levels of customer collaboration. In adaptive systems, though, it's more than important: It's absolutely essential.

7. Philosophizing!

In Agile, the customer has to collaborate with you all the time when you're constantly specifying new requirements and asking them to check the increments and give you feedback. If they don't do this, you won't be able to adapt.

Comparing customer collaboration with contract negotiation may not be fair, as they are two separate aspects. In an ideal Agile project with a time-and-material contract, no contract negotiation is needed, and the customer and supplier can enjoy their collaborative relationship. However, if one forces an Agile project to use a fixed-price contract, all those contract negotiations will return.

In other words, whether or not we can remove contract negotiations mainly depends on the contract type, rather than the development approach. Nevertheless, it's worth mentioning that it's easier to have a time-and-material contract for an Agile project compared to a predictive one.

7.4.4 Statement #4

> We value responding to change over following a plan.

This statement, similar to the second one, is specific to adaptive systems. Rather than having a predictive, upfront plan that can show us the way, we are dependent on adaptation. The latter is usually referred to as "change" in Agile, probably because it makes customers happy to know they are free to change everything, but in fact, it's not a change unless it doesn't match the initial baselined plan, which we don't have in adaptive systems. Technically, what we have is a continuous stream of new ideas. However, let's keep calling them changes, just for the sake of all the customers out there.

7.4.5 The Principles

The Agile Manifesto is pleasantly short. However, the authors thought it might be a good idea to elaborate on the newly named Agile idea, so they created the following 12 principles.

7.4.5.1 Principle #1

> Our highest priority is to satisfy the customer through early and continuous delivery of valuable software.

After all, we're doing business, and we need to have happy customers. That's obvious. However, nowadays we prefer to say that the end-users' satisfaction is the ultimate measure because that generates profit for the customer and, sooner or later, will satisfy the customer in a sustainable way.

So, how do we satisfy them? That's by the software we create, which has the potential to generate value (e.g., money). When we deliver early and continuously, we will generate the value sooner, and we also have the opportunity to adapt and create something that the market really wants and will pay for, rather than something that we expect them to want.

7.4.5.2 Principle #2

> Welcome changing requirements, even late in development. Agile processes harness change for the customer's competitive advantage.

There's no harm in putting more effort into marketing our flexibility toward change!

7.4.5.3 Principle #3

> Deliver working software frequently, from a couple of weeks to a couple of months, with a preference to the shorter timescale.

"Delivery" can refer to the releasable increments we build into our iterations, as well as actual releases that are made available to the end-users. This principle is about the former and suggests having short iterations on the one hand, and done, usable, releasable increments on the other.

7.4.5.4 Principle #4

> Business people and developers must work together daily throughout the project.

This goes against the idea of separating the business people (customer or otherwise) from the technical people, which is still a problem in projects. They sometimes see each other as enemies, which is not the best thing that can happen in a project.

In addition to that, we can't adapt if the business people are not available all the time. Think about the continuous analysis of new features and testing of the completed units.

7.4.5.5 Principle #5

> Build projects around motivated individuals. Give them the environment and support they need, and trust them to get the job done.

Instead of giving detailed instruction to people, support them, motivate them, and trust them, and let them self-organize and find their way.

7.4.5.6 Principle #6

> The most efficient and effective method of conveying information to and within a development team is face-to-face conversation.

Agile methods have a preference for face-to-face conversations (instead of, e.g., emailing). Face-to-face communications can be effective when done properly, such as those defined in Scrum with defined agendas and timeboxing, but they can be a waste of time if not managed properly.

7.4.5.7 Principle #7

> Working software is the primary measure of progress.

Most projects measure the wrong things. It's a fundamental problem because what you measure is what you get. If you measure how many lines of code are produced, you will just get more lines of code. If you measure how busy the developers are, you will get busier developers. If you measure velocity, you will get higher velocity (which is not the goal).

So, what should be measured? The main measure is the amount of value generated, and how much closer we've got to the project goals.

7.4.5.8 Principle #8

> Agile processes promote sustainable development. The sponsors, developers, and users should be able to maintain a constant pace indefinitely.

No over-over-time work before releases. It's about maximizing value in the long term. It's not about short-term gains that may lead to a lower production rate and lower quality in the long run.

7.4.5.9 Principle #9

> Continuous attention to technical excellence and good design enhances agility.

There's a risk of having poor design in adaptive systems because design is done gradually instead of upfront. Practices such as refactoring help solve this problem, as well as process considerations such as having a proper definition of done.

7.4.5.10 Principle #10

> Simplicity – the art of maximizing the amount of work not done – is essential.

This is a complicated way of saying that having more features is not always a good thing.

It's a good idea to keep the solution simple and have only the really useful features in it because it saves time and money (which can be used for other projects) and reduces the maintenance costs.

7.4.5.11 Principle #11

> The best architectures, requirements, and designs emerge from self-organizing teams.

Instead of being worried about the direction of the project, you should authorize the team members and trust their judgement.

7.4.5.12 Principle #12

> At regular intervals, the team reflects on how to become more effective, then tunes and adjusts its behavior accordingly.

You need to accept that the way you work is not perfect, but that you can always improve it in small steps.

About the Author

Nader K. Rad started working with projects in 1996: first, as a project planner in construction projects, and then in large process-plant projects. In parallel, he was also involved in IT projects and startups.

He gradually moved from project planning into the wider project management domain by helping project managers and companies improve their project, program, and portfolio management systems.

Nowadays, he spends most of his time contributing to standards and methods – he's been the co-author of P3.express, NUPP, and the seventh edition of the PMBOK® Guide, and the official reviewer of PRINCE2®, PRINCE2 Agile®, and MSP®. The rest of his time is spent presenting at conferences and developing eLearning courses in their company, Management Plaza.

More information: https://nader.pm and gemini://nader.pm

Index

-
40-hour work week 69

A
acceptance test 88
adaptive approach 4, 13
adaptive system 4
affinity estimation 86
Agile Manifesto 115
artifacts 36, 51

B
Brooks' law 16
burn-down bar 61
burn-down chart 32, 59
burn-up chart 58
bus factor 66
business as usual (operations) 10

C
Cargo Cult effect 10
Chief Product Owner 48
Cockburn, Alistair 53
Cockburn Scale 53
coding standards 68
coffee cup (planning poker) 85
collective code ownership 66

co-located team 54
component team 47
continuous integration 67, 68
contract, fixed-price 96
      dynamic-scope 96
      fixed-scope 96
cross-functionality 17, 23
Crystal 53
Crystal Clear 53
cumulative flow diagram 63
customer bill of rights 105
cycle 7

D
daily routine 65
Daily Scrum 15, 31, 50
day planning 89
Definition of Done 36, 45, 52
Definition of Ready 30
deliverable 7
Developer 23, 47
development timebox (DSDM) 95
DSDM 46, 91, 110

E
empowerment 109
epic user stories (epics) 41

escaped defect 57
estimating 74
events, timeboxed 24
exception (DSDM) 95
expected product 95
eXtreme Programming (XP) 14, 65, 105

F
facilitation 21
feature teams 47
feedback loop 87
fixed-duration iteration 5
fixed-price, fixed-scope 96
fixed-scope iteration 5
framework 13
frequent release 54

G
generic development lifecycle 2
Grow-and-Split 48

I
ideal product 95
ideal-time 74
Increment 7, 27, 36, 44, 52
incremental delivery 4
information radiators 55
information visualization 56
Internal Rate of Return (IRR) 40
INVEST 72
IT development 9
iteration 7, 88
    duration of 5
    planning 89
    timeboxed 6
iterative development 4

K
Kanban 63, 97
Kanban board 97

L
LeSS™ 46

M
minimum acceptable product 94
MoSCoW prioritization 94
MoV® 39
MSP® 10

N
Nearly Universal Principles of
    Projects 79
Net Present Value (NPV) 40
Nexus Integration Team 49
Nexus™ 46
Niko-Niko calendar 63
Nowadays (XP) 55

O
osmotic communication 54
overall plan 106

P
P3.express 7
pair negotiation 88
pair programming 65, 88
Payback Period 40
plan-driven development 3
Planning Onion 89
planning poker 82
PMBOK® Guide 7
portfolio 10
predictive lifecycle 3
PRINCE2® 7, 111
Product Backlog 14, 36, 42
    grooming 41
    refinement 41
Product Goal 15, 28, 34, 36, 37
Product Owner 15, 19, 42, 48
product planning 89
programmer bill of rights 107
programs 10
progress information 58
progress toward the Sprint Goal 31
project constraints triangle 92
projects 9

Q
quality 8

R
re-estimating 87
refactoring 68
release 88
    of product to production 46
release planning 89
Return on Investment (ROI) 40

S
SAFe™ 46
Scaled Scrum 16, 46
Schwaber, Ken 13
Scrum 13, 113
    events 24
    roles 47
Scrum Guide 13
Scrum Master 15, 21, 22, 48
Scrum of Scrums 50
Scrum@Scale™ 46
Scrum Team 15
    attributes and rules 16
    members roles 16
    roles 18
self-management 17
self-organization 17, 109
simple design 66
spiking 70
Split-and-Seed 48
Sprint (Scrum) 14, 25, 49
Sprint Backlog 14, 25, 26, 36, 42, 52
Sprint Goal 26, 28, 36, 42, 43
Sprint Planning 15, 27, 49
Sprint Retrospective 15, 25, 35, 51
Sprint Review 15, 25, 33, 51
Sprint Zero 26
stakeholders 15
stand-up meeting 69
story points 76
Sutherland, Jeff 13

T
technical debt 68
test-driven development 67
test-first development 67
themes 41
timebox 5
Total Cost of Ownership (TCO) 40
Tracker 69
triangulation 85
triangulation board 86
T-shaped skill set 23
T-shirt sizes 78

U
unit test 88
upfront planning 93
user story 72

V
velocity 75, 77
virtual team 31

W
walking skeleton 55
waterfall systems 3
Work in progress (WIP) 97, 98

Y
yesterday's weather 79